QUESTIONS GREAT FINANCIAL ADVISORS ASK

. . . AND INVESTORS NEED TO KNOW

QUESTIONS GREAT FINANCIAL ADVISORS ASK

. . . AND INVESTORS NEED TO KNOW

Alan Parisse
and David Richman

KAPLAN PUBLISHING

President, Kaplan Publishng: Roy Lipner
Vice President and Publisher: Maureen McMahon
Vice President, Financial and Custom Publishing: Cynthia A. Zigmund
Senior Managing Editor: Jack Kiburz
Cover Designer: Scott Rattray, Rattray Design
Typesetter: Janet Schroeder

Published by Kaplan Publishing,
a division of Kaplan, Inc.

Printed in the United States of America

08 10 9 8 7 6 5 4

Library of Congress Cataloging-in-Publication Data

Parisse, Alan.
Questions great financial advisors ask—and investors need to know/Alan Parisse and David Richman.
p. cm.
Includes bibliographical references and index.
ISBN-13: 978-1-4195-2680-0
ISBN-10: 1-4195-2680-4
1. Investment advisor-client relationships. 2. Investment advisors. I. Richman, David. II. Title.
HG4621.P367 2006
332.6'2–dc22

2006010542

DEDICATION

To our wives, Lisa and Faigie, who had a question of their own: "When is that book *going to be completed so we can have our weekends back?" And to Alanna, Jason, Ryan, who for many years have taught us both the value of asking questions.*

Acknowledgments

Our heartfelt thanks to the scores of advisors and industry leaders who have had such a positive impact on our lives and careers. A special thanks to all those who are quoted in the book and to the many others whose compliance departments were unable to get back to us by the deadline. Particular thanks go to all the financial advisors, mentors, colleagues, and friends whose ideas and thoughts contributed so much to us, including:

Steve Booren, Alan Breedlove, Dewey Bushaw, Lee Carlin, Charles Carvette III, Jody Chadwick, Bob Cogan, Michael Cooper, Stephen DiCarlo, Jim Durocher, Bill Dwyer, David Ferris, Marc Fischer, Mary Fleishmann, Dick Friedland, Carol Ann Fulmer, Bob Green, Richard Grund, Catherine Hanks, Mark Harper, Jeff Hayes, Tom Healey, Hill Jason, Andy Kalbaugh, Tom Lewis, Tim Marinec, David Mattia, Ross Mayer, Paul McCauley, Tom McConnell, Gary McGuirk, Bill McIntosh, Frank Patzke, John Rafal, G.G. Robins, Mark Rogers, Henry Sampers, Guy Staples, Dick Sumberg, Jerry Vainisi, Lori Van Dusen, Heather Walsh, Jane Westberg, Dick Wollack, and Porsche Young.

Last but by no means least, our deep appreciation to Nan Spires, who championed and managed this project, Mary Good, who commissioned it, Cynthia Zigmund, who made it a reality, and Susan J. Marks, whose energy and skill brought it to completion.

Contents

Introduction

As a financial advisor, would you like to:

- Understand and serve your clients better?
- Create clients for life?
- Generate passionate advocates for your financial advice?
- Dramatically boost closing ratios?

Questions Great Financial Advisors Ask can help you do all this and more.

Great financial advising in the 21st century isn't about transactions or developing the perfect personality, sales pitch, and crushing close. It's about learning what it takes to advise clients based on an in-depth understanding of their financial needs, wants, hopes, and dreams. The real service that you as a financial advisor offer in today's Internet-centric world isn't the "product." It's you and your ability to truly make a difference in your clients' lives. It's the questions you ask rather than the products you recommend that ultimately distinguish you in the marketplace and significantly bolster your bottom line.

This book contains no preset conversations or sales scripts. Chances are you're already overloaded with those, and they don't tend to work anyway. Instead, this book will help you take a new look at and recharge your professional approach to working with clients. In these pages you will learn the questions great advisors ask that lead to the probing and personal conversations necessary to diagnose and understand clients'—and potential clients'—deep-seated feelings about money. Dealing with each client's unique investment personality or "wiring" is what ultimately determines your success or failure as an advisor.

In the following pages, you'll meet and learn better how to relate to "the Putterer," who enjoys playing with his or her investments; "Paul Perfect," who already knows everything and wonders why in the world he is talking to you; stingy "Ms. Pennywise," who thinks every fee is much too much; and "the Cynic," who doubts everything anyone says. As you will see, these all-too-familiar personalities can block your efforts to understand a prospective client's true feelings about and toward money and investing. Not being able to "read" your clients can end up derailing even the best financial planning. This book, with its direction and ideas, can empower you to better understand your prospects and clients and help guide them around the often emotional obstacles that can thwart their financial success.

Most investment mistakes are driven by emotional missteps, not intellectual ones. Great advisors can wring the emotion out of client decision making.

For investors, this book can help you identify your own investment personality. Armed with that knowledge, you can learn how to capitalize on your financial strengths and overcome your investment weaknesses.

Throughout this book, you'll periodically see lists of questions, suggestions, and stories from some of North America's top financial advisors. Chapter Six summarizes and expands on the questions in the book. They're organized by topic for ease of use. Some advisors are quoted directly by name; for others, pseudonyms were used and still others are composites of the authors' experiences and those of the many advisors they have known. We hope you find all the suggestions valuable.

Coauthors David Richman and Alan Parisse are well qualified to help advisors and investors come out ahead.

Investment industry veteran David Richman is a managed-accounts specialist for one of the nation's premier investment companies. During his nearly 30-year career in the financial industry, he has participated in more than 4,000 in-depth meetings with high-net-worth individuals, families, and institutions. He has been a featured speaker at scores of affluent-investor seminars and has counseled hundreds of investment advisors, many of whom consider him a valued coach and confidant.

Richman has been a successful securities retailer, wholesaler, and principal. He's also the coauthor of *This Is Your Time: Empowering Today's Financial Advisor.* Richman holds a BA and an MA from the University of Rochester and a JD from the University of Connecticut.

Alan Parisse has been informing and inspiring financial advisors for three decades. He's a renowned speaker who, over the years, has counted among his clients many of the world's top financial services organizations, including the Securities Industry Association, the Investment Company Institute, and the Million Dollar Round Table.

He's the first and only speaker from the investment business to be inducted into the National Speakers Association's Hall of Fame. Parisse's ideas have been cited in *the Wall Street Journal, BusinessWeek,* and *Barron's.* He has written or coauthored numerous books and audiotapes, including *This is Your Time: Empowering Today's Financial Advisor, Power Marketing: 101 Best Financial Marketing Ideas*, and *The Great Salesperson: The Ultimate Guide to Influencing Others.*

Parisse holds a BS from the State University of New York at Buffalo and an MBA from the University of Arizona.

Together with the great advisors in this book, they can help put you on the path to great advising. So, if you're ready, turn the page and get started on your journey with them.

Prologue

Great advisors diagnose and celebrate individuality. They realize that everyone has the right to personal feelings about their money, what they want to do with it, and why. They help individual clients make the right financial decisions for themselves and their families.

We hope the suggestions, tips, and personal stories in this book are valuable to you and help you better serve your clients, no matter what their situations or idiosyncrasies. All of us can become better at what we do with the right approach and the right questions, and listening to how people answer those questions.

As financial services has evolved from transaction-centric to client-centric, those who embraced the change and became passionate true believers in the client-centric approach report a positive difference in their closing ratios, retention rates, and personal satisfaction from the contributions they make to their clients' lives. If you haven't joined them already, do it now.

Keep in mind that people of all ages and financial situations today need caring, knowledgeable advisors of all kinds to help them deal with the complexities of modern life. They want and need the caring and knowledgeable doctor to help them navigate the medical maze; an equally qualified lawyer to ward off or resolve legal problems; and just as qualified an accountant to plot their course through the tax system. The majority also need a similarly expert financial advisor to simplify their financial lives and help them identify and achieve their visions of their financial future. The opportunity has never been greater for financial advisors who put their clients first. Your clients and prospects need you now more than ever. They need you to take an active role in understanding their "investment wiring" and their individual circumstances, purposes, and goals, and then to take a stand and tell them what you think is the best course of action for them.

You can do that by asking questions and truly listening to your clients and prospects. In these pages, we've tried to guide you on the best way to do that.

Whatever you do, though, don't lose sight of the tried-and-true practices of great advisors:

- Get on your clients' side of the table and let them know you're there.
- Ask the right questions. That's what will distinguish you as an advisor. And never be afraid to ask the logical follow-up or the tough question.
- Listen actively not only to how your clients answer your questions but to the subtext of their answers. Pay attention to the spoken and unspoken words, and don't let your mind wander.
- Understand each client's unique investment wiring–how he or she truly feels about money. Go beyond the obvious. Help all of your clients identify the purpose for their money, and then help them set and strive for their goals.
- Diagnose the person and the situation completely before prescribing. Don't rush to solutions before you're sure of the issues.
- Respect your client's point of view. Remember that everyone is entitled to their opinion. While you, as an advisor, can and should disagree with a client's position when needed, always honor and respect him or her as an individual.
- Temper the financial-media chatter with reality, and take the emotion out of investment decisions. That's perhaps the greatest service an advisor can provide clients.
- Take a stand. Great advisors are not just "yes" people; they don't just tell their clients what they want to hear. Tell your clients what you really think, and then go beyond simply asking for the order. Tell them the best action for their unique, individual situations. That's

what great doctors do, and that's what you as a great advisor should do, too.
- Treat clients as your honored guests, but let them know the house rules. That means don't hang on to clients who sap your soul and your strength. Great advisors know that not everyone is the right client for them.
- Be proud of your contribution to your clients and to society. Yours is important work.
- Be lofty in defining your powerful and unique value proposition, and then be true to that proposition.
- To truly discover your client's investment wiring, go beyond asking questions. Gather as much information as you can—whether from observing interactions with his or her spouse to making note of the cars in the driveway. There is so much information, so many variables, and so many options that most people are overwhelmed and confused about investing. You can help your clients best by knowing as much about them as possible.

People today are simply "thought flooded" and cannot process all the financial and investing information that bombards them daily. Yet one of the predominant ways advisors complete a presentation is to sit back and say something like, "Well, what do you think?"

Does it make sense to ask someone who is overwhelmed with the options, confused by the jargon, and unsure of the next step what he or she thinks? If you ask clients, chances are they will respond by saying, "I think I need to think about it." Then they may think they need to think about it forever. If they don't get a headache from all the thinking, you will.

Of course, a great doctor wouldn't merely ask patients what they think. He or she would go out on a limb and tell patients what in the world the doctor thinks they should do. As a financial professional, you should do the same. Once you know your clients' situation fully and understand their investment wiring, it is time to tell them what you, as a professional, think they should do. Instead of asking "What do you think?" try this question: "Do you know what you should do?" Most people will say "no" or "no, what?" Then you tell them.

As a great advisor, don't ever lose sight of the fact that today, dispensing advice is about truly making a difference in your clients' lives. With the right tools and commitment, you can advise clients based on an in-depth understanding of their financial needs, wants, hopes, and dreams. Remember, it's the questions you ask rather than the products you recommend that ultimately distinguish you in the marketplace.

Chapter

1

WHAT MAKES A GREAT FINANCIAL ADVISOR?

Personality, product pitches, and a crushing close aren't enough when it comes to financial advising today. Investors, after all, don't need a financial advisor to obtain current market information, trade stocks and bonds, or buy a host of financial products. In today's Internet-wired world, the product investors really want–and the service great financial advisors provide–is the ability to help them define and then achieve their financial goals and dreams.

It's certainly no secret that the financial-advice business has changed. Executing transactions has become a low-price/low-value commodity. Advice, however, continues to be ever more valuable and in demand. Moreover, advisors who get to know their clients better are in a position to provide them with a wider array of services, which means more business and a greater probability of client loyalty over the long haul. Ever since the financial services industry began studying client loyalty decades ago, the message has been clear: the more services a client uses, the more likely he or she is to remain a client.

Yet some advisors still are reluctant to take the steps necessary to change their business model. That's understandable; change is challenging. Moreover, change can take time, and time means money. As Jed, a 30-something advisor from Dallas, puts it: "My firm is pushing us to move quickly to an advice-driven, fee-based practice. I know it will pay off in the long run. The question is, 'Will I make it to the long run?' After all, the kids need braces, and the mortgage needs to be paid right now."

"Here's the big issue," says Dan, an advisor in the same office who is in his 50s and has considerably more experience under his belt. "Not only does it take a lot of time to convert a transaction-oriented client relationship into a fee-based advisory relationship, but there is a risk of losing that client's business you already have. It can take months to convince them that the change is to their benefit, and they might just get turned off and go elsewhere."

Dan complains that in trying to adopt this fee-based approach, his income has slipped, his sales cycles are longer, and his closing ratios lower. Dan's experience is not unique. During the transition from a transaction-based to fee-based approach, income may drop for a while before it stabilizes and annuitizes. Nonetheless, advisors who have enthusiastically accepted the fee-based model are capitalizing on their new approach. In fact, many say that after a short adjustment period, sales cycles are comparable, closing ratios improve, and, as they offer more services, their wallet share increases. In addition, client loyalty is strengthened and, as a result, referrals rise.

Perhaps Dan should examine his underlying attitude. Something is undermining his ability to transition to the new business model. Like many successful advisors accustomed to doing business the old way, Dan is finding it tough to let go of what has worked in the past. So, while he intellectually understands all the arguments for moving from transactions to advice, he still needs to convince himself emotionally. Once he does that, his closing and conversion ratios should improve dramatically.

CLIENT FOCUS

Good financial advisors become great ones by learning to be client-centric financial experts who not only master the technical side of the craft but offer advice based on a deep understanding of each client's financial wants, needs, hopes, and dreams. As an advisor today, you ultimately distinguish yourself in the marketplace by the questions you ask and the relationships you nurture rather than the products you recommend.

Think about dispensing financial and investment advice as comparable to the way the best doctors offer medical advice. Those physicians, no matter how busy, make the time to ask their patients about their lives, families, and feelings. Doctors don't ask such questions just to be nice, and they don't do it to make small talk. They gently ask probing questions because they know they cannot diagnose or treat a patient without understanding more than just his or her vital signs and test results. They also must understand the context of that patient's life to provide the best possible treatment and solution to the problem at hand.

For financial advisors' interactions with clients, the goal is to establish a long-term relationship, not just a one-time quick sale. As with doctors, financial advisors cannot diagnose accurately or treat properly without understanding more than a mere balance sheet or what seems apparent from quick answers to stock questions. Great advisors know they must understand the context within which their clients invest. They know that long-term, in-depth client relationships come from fully understanding each client's attitudes and emotions about, and experiences with, money.

Lori Van Dusen, one of the nation's most successful advisors, credits much of her success to what she calls "emotional smarts." Named to *Barron's* 2005 list of the top 100 financial advisors, Van Dusen is a member of Van Dusen, Mattia & Cooper, a Smith Barney team that oversees $2.5 billion in assets.

"Every client is different," Van Dusen says, "so I focus on reading each situation to determine precisely when to ask the right question in just the right way. While I'm very gentle with some and direct with others, my first objective is always the same: I want to find out what they want to do in their lives."

Paul McCauley and Gary McGuirk head a Private Wealth Advisory team for Merrill Lynch in Boston, Massachusetts. They provide guidance to clients with approximately $1 billion in assets.

"Wealthy people hate to be pitched," says McCauley. "Their sales radar is off the charts."

Rather than begin new client meetings by pitching their services or some hot product, great advisors–including McCauley and McGuirk–start with a question such as, "How can I help you?" They work hard at listening to and understanding what matters to their clients and prospects. Then they can provide the right advice for each unique circumstance. In turn, their advice helps the client make the right decision, even when that choice lies outside the client's normal realm of comfort. We call this kind of communication *emotional eloquence.*

"It's important, also," says Van Dusen, "to be willing to ask the uncomfortable question when necessary." Great advisors ask the hard questions and tell clients not only what they want to hear, but what they need to hear. This level of communication is particularly important when dealing with clients and prospects whose wealth is concentrated in a single stock to which they have an emotional attachment.

The information technology boom of the late 1990s created instant millionaires and billionaires at an unprecedented rate. For many, mega financial losses or ruin occurred just as quickly when the Internet bubble burst. Even some of the nation's top billionaires took a hit. In 1999 and 2000, Bill Gates saw his shares in Microsoft fall some 60 percent, costing him $51 billion of the $84 billion he had at the beginning of 1999. Michael Dell's holdings in his company, Dell Computer Corporation, fell some 65 percent, and Amazon.com founder Jeff Bezos's shares in Amazon sank 77 percent. None of these leaders missed any meals, but all would have benefited from more diversification.

People with concentrated wealth often are reluctant to sell any of their beloved stock despite historically low capital gains rates and an array of investment vehicles and strategies that offer tax-favored diversification. The then chief executive of JP Morgan Private Bank, Maria Elena Lagomasino, put it this way in *Forbes* on October 11, 2004: "The biggest land mine to avoid in staying rich . . . is overconcentration in a particular investment . . . A single stock position has a less than 50 percent probability of sustaining wealth over 20 years. But a diversified portfolio increases the probability to 85 percent."

Even with these kinds of statistics, clients often stubbornly refuse to diversify because the attachment to their stock is emotional, not intellectual. After all, in most cases it was the stock that helped make them rich in the first place. Nonetheless, it's essential to show them the numbers. Remember, a great advisor cannot be a simple yes-man.

McCauley and McGuirk recount the story of a client who was the only one of 12 senior executives at a technology company who remained wealthy after the bust. All 12 had financial advisors, but apparently none of those advising the other 11 executives was willing to stand up to his client and persuade him or her to diversify away from investing solely in the company. Perhaps those advisors were afraid of losing the accounts; perhaps not. Whatever the reason, it appears that "They didn't tell their clients what they needed to hear, just what they wanted to hear," says McGuirk.

Telling clients what they need to hear in a manner they can accept requires deep personal understanding–emotional eloquence–and it's not easy.

Pointing out other cases and statistics rarely persuades a client to sell significant amounts of the beloved stock. Sometimes you'll fail to persuade the client to sell any stock at all. You may dramatize the point by running Monte Carlo simulations, but the client still may refuse to budge. Again, the attachment is emotional, not intellectual, and requires a thoughtful approach.

"We had to be careful in standing up to our client, "says McGuirk. "We had to be 'antiseptic' about it. This company and this stock was his baby."

So McCauley and McGuirk removed the personal context from discussions with the technology executive about the company and its stock. Instead of *your* stock or *your* company, it was *a* stock or *a* company. Such objectivity helped to turn the conversations into needs- and goals-based discussions. In that context, the concept of diversification didn't need to be sold; it was obvious. As it turned out, that approach saved much of their client's fortune.

THE ADVISOR'S MOTIVATION

The mission of helping clients protect their financial assets and achieve their dreams is paramount. Great advisors serve first, putting clients' interests ahead of their own. There's that client-centric approach again.

Financial advisors who brag about their own financial successes while their clients suffer financial losses doesn't cut it. Nor does the office filled with sales awards and plaques. Such trophies and mementoes are validating and ego-gratifying, but what some people call an "I-love-me wall" doesn't convey that all-important client-centric message. After all, success shouldn't be measured by gross commissions or the transaction of the moment. Instead, a financial advisor's success should be a natural outgrowth of providing financial advice that helps clients not only protect their assets but understand and fulfill their financial goals. Imagine walking into a doctor's office that has sales awards from drug companies posted on the walls. We all expect to see evidence of an individual's credentials, and in the case of a doctor, maybe even framed patient testimonials. Consider what your clients think when they see what's on your walls, and for that matter, what's in your magazine rack.

All that said, financial advising is a business, not a charity. It is a highly skilled profession that bears the burden of responsibility for the financial welfare of clients and their families. As a result, significant financial rewards for a job well done are important and appropriate for an advisor. The good news is that the great advisors who take the right approach to working with their clients will indeed reap significant rewards. They will have a consistent and growing income stream that is not tied to the transaction of the moment but to the building of client relationships and the delivery of ongoing advice. They can have the sales awards and the financial benefits, and their clients will profit, too.

Advisors who use their clients' success as their measure of achievement can indeed realize their own financial dreams. Imagine never again fretting about generating business. Imagine a continuous stream of high-net-worth referrals coming to you. Chances are you would be extremely satisfied with your numbers, your client relationships, and your chosen profession.

Harold is a 76-year-old financial advisor with a massive book of business. Why does he keep working?

"A long time ago when I first started out, I really made a difference in a client family's life," says Harold. "It made me understand that this business is about helping people. That's what made me a success, and that's why I still do it."

Perhaps that approach also explains why Harold continues to attract a bevy of young clients. He knows how to listen and is fully committed to helping clients achieve their financial goals. Harold's client-centric approach to dispensing financial advice is like that of the previously mentioned physician who provides sound medical advice. Neither Harold nor a good physician relies on one-size-fits-all questions. They tailor their questions to each specific individual and his or her situation.

THE FALLACY OF QUESTIONNAIRES

The financial advisory industry is awash in standard questionnaires with boilerplate questions designed to keep compliance departments happy. Admittedly, many of the questions make sense. Tangible facts such as family demographics, the assets clients possess, and where they have those assets are important. Few investors really comprehend the other, more subjective questions, however. Consequently, their answers are of little value. "What is your risk tolerance?" is an essential question, for example, but few people actually understand the meaning of the words "risk" or "tolerance"–let alone what those words mean in combination when applied to investing. As a result, a client's answer to a typical questionnaire about risk tolerance often reveals very little about his or her underlying feelings and attitudes toward money and investing.

Those underlying feelings and attitudes are part of a person's *investment wiring.* An advisor must recognize a client's or prospect's investment wiring to provide the best advice. Unfortunately, some advisors believe that simply by looking at the answers on a standard questionnaire, they are able to understand their client's investment wiring. That's rarely true. Even though questionnaires are almost always supplemented with an in-person interview, misperceptions can occur. (We'll talk more about *investment wiring* in Chapter 3.)

Bill, a financial advisor in San Diego, targeted as a client Joe, 64, and his $5.5 million portfolio. In his two earlier meetings, Joe had put on quite a performance that conveyed an expectation of big risks and big rewards. As a result, Bill pegged Joe as an aggressive investor who wanted to take risks and reap commensurate rewards. For this day's meeting in Joe's opulent offices overlooking the Pacific Ocean, Bill had prepared a proposal tailored to his prospective client's apparent bold persona. Certain that the advisory relationship was sealed and that the meeting was little more than a formality, Bill brought along two younger colleagues to observe an easy closing.

Twenty minutes and several pie charts into his presentation, Bill noticed that he had lost Joe's interest. "You seem a bit distant. Have we missed something?" he asked.

Joe not only didn't like the proposed strategy, but the 75 percent allocation to equities with a good chunk in small caps and emerging markets actually repulsed him. "I didn't tell you this last time," he said, "but I watched my father die penniless because he invested too aggressively. He lost his money and his manhood, and that's not going to happen to me!"

So much for diagnosing prospective clients based on questionnaires and early impressions. Bill thought he had figured out what Joe wanted, but he had failed to look beyond the façade. Bill fell into the trap that some mental health professionals call the "presenting problem." That's when a patient presents himself one way but in reality is quite another. Bill didn't bother to ask the probing questions or take the time to get past the way Joe presented himself to discover Joe's *investment wiring*. The result: Bill never got the account.

CLIENT CONNECTIONS

Great advisors must know their stuff, yet this technical knowledge is only the table stakes–it's essential to play the game, but not sufficient to play it well. The real difference between an ordinary advisor and a great one is, as we've mentioned, client-centricity as opposed to transaction-centricity. The great advisor is a master communicator. He or she listens deeply to what clients have to say and then really hears their answers.

Denver-based Steve Booren, a top advisor with LPL Financial Services, knows the value of putting relationships first. "I start every prospective client interview with the point of view that I will take nothing less than a great relationship. Then I make sure our personalities, style, and substance fit," he explains. For those who doubt the efficacy of Booren's approach: he has more than 550 satisfied referral-only clients to prove it.

Dick Sumberg, of The Financial Advisors, runs a $300 million practice in Andover, Massachusetts. A longtime leader with Jefferson Pilot Financial, he talks proudly about all his clients being his good friends. Instead of going to work, he says he sees himself as simply visiting with his friends. "Most of them didn't start as friends," but he says, "from the beginning I explain that my goal is to become an integral part of their big life decisions. To do that, I need to become a part of the fabric of their lives. While I make it clear that I don't expect to come to dinner every week, I let them know that I plan on having a metaphorical seat at their table."

In the initial interview, Sumberg says he explains to prospective clients, "The purpose of this meeting is for you to 'kick my tires,' and for us to see if we have a good rapport. If not, that doesn't make you or me bad. It will just mean we are not a good fit."

Over the years, he adds, he's learned there's no point in working with people he doesn't want to get to know better. "I will not waste energy on people who don't interest me."

Having a great relationship, however, doesn't mean engaging in too much idle chitchat, especially early on. Be cognizant of wasting your client's time, and yours. Whenever possible, steer the conversations with your clients and prospects to substantive issues. Remember that you are present in a professional capacity. Think like the good physician who steers clear of chatting about the weather or other irrelevancies. He or she gets down to work, and so should you. The focus of conversations should be on serious topics that might be relevant to understanding a client's or prospect's investment wiring. It is usually more fruitful to ask a client how he or she built his or her business, career, or practice; how the client goes about choosing advisors; or who he or she relies on for advice as opposed to talking about the golf or tennis game or the marathon the client just played or ran.

All that said, however, don't rule out social pleasantries and small talk as a way to get to know your clients. Banter can yield important connections. Learning that you both have a passion for golf or some other sport can create a connection. So can discovering that both your daughter and your client's daughter hang out in Aspen skiing, are medical students at UCLA, or ride horses. It may seem innocuous and meaningless on the surface, but in today's society, where many of us have drifted far from family and childhood friends, we often put a high value on even the illusion of common ground. This kind of a connection can create a quick bond between you and your client or prospect.

Jennifer, an eager 30-something advisor in Chicago, struggled to connect with a wealthy prospect. She and Margaret seemed to have nothing in common. One day they ran into each other in a restaurant. Margaret, noticing that Jennifer was eating jambalaya, mentioned that it had been her father's favorite dish. "He was a New Orleans native," she added. Surprised, Jennifer replied that her grandfather had been the opera conductor there. Margaret's jaw dropped. "What was his name?" she asked. It turns out that Margaret's father was a businessman whose first love had been opera. He had been a singer in Jennifer's father's chorus! It's no surprise that Jennifer got the account.

Small talk can yield additional information. Jim, an advisor in Wellesley, Massachusetts, was visiting a prospect, a couple whose home was undergoing extensive masonry work. "That's really attractive," Jim said. "Are you happy with the contractor?" The husband merely said, "Yes." The wife, on the other hand, quickly volunteered to pass on the contractor's name and number. As a result, Jim made a mental note to remember that she would be the more likely of the couple to refer others to him.

When you engage in small talk, don't allow yourself to drift too far, however. In all likelihood, your clients and prospects have enough friends already. They need advice much more than a new best friend. So stay on purpose.

Well managed, small talk can yield valuable insights. Poorly managed, it can be a waste of time. Don't end up like many advisors, who, on leaving a meeting with a prospect, think they've laid the foundation for a great relationship only to learn later that the client signed on with another advisor.

As soon as Tom walked into prospective client Don's office his face lit up. "That's a beautiful northern pike you have on the wall. Where did you catch it?"

"Georgian Bay up in Ontario," proud angler Don replied. That could have served as an excellent connection between the two and segued into getting to know the client. Instead, Tom allowed the conversation to turn into a 45-minute discussion about fishing in eastern Canadian lakes. Before Tom could figure out how to get the meeting back on track, Don ran out of time. Tom may have found himself a new fishing buddy, but he didn't establish the level of respect needed to create a professional relationship between the two men.

The Value of Small Talk

Things you can discover while talking small:

- Is the person someone who could provide good referrals?
- Are they do-it-yourselfers or do they hire professionals for advice (decorators, tutors, painters, plumbers, etc.)?
- How do they interact with other professionals?
- How do they hire other types of professionals? Do they rely on independent research, friends, and family, or do they go with big-name firms? Do they take the first name they see in the Yellow Pages or in a Google search?
- When it comes to major purchases such as automobiles, do they buy based on quality, price, reputation, relationship, convenience, or something else?
- Are they impulsive buyers or do they deliberate first?
- What are their attitudes toward their family?
- Are they open or stubborn when it comes to opinion and direction from others?
- Do they delegate or prefer total control?
- Are they loyal or fickle when it comes to others, especially advisors?

ASK THE RIGHT QUESTIONS

If a conversation or small talk gets away from substantive issues, as happened between Tom and Don, asking the right questions can get it back on track. For example, five minutes into their passionate fishing conversation, Tom could have said, "Don, obviously we can talk about fishing forever, and I hope we get a chance to do that someday, but let's get back on track. Why are we here today? How can I help you?"

Great financial advisors are great listeners, too. The fuel for great listening is asking the right questions. That means following up with more questions that steer conversations toward relevant substance and, when necessary, to the next level of client understanding.

A good opening question for a client or prospect might be, "How do you make investment decisions?" That person's answer could range from reading the newspaper or watching television to talking to family and friends to careful analysis and perhaps even to hunches and intuition. Whatever the answer, though, as an advisor listen to it, ask more questions, and probe the whys and hows of the answer. Those answers should tell you plenty about that individual's attitudes about his or her money, how he or she has tended to make past decisions, the extent that emotions entered into these decisions, whether he or she was rational in making the decisions, and whether a consistent discipline entered into the process.

Compare the quality of the information garnered by the cardiologist who merely asks the patient if he or she exercises regularly with that of the physician who follows up the first question and probes further. "Do you ride a bike?" If so, "What type, mountain or road?" "How often?" "How many miles?" "Do you do a lot of hill work?" "Do you enjoy it or do it for some other reason?" "Is it because your spouse pesters you about exercise?" "Does he or she pester you a lot?" One question naturally leads to another, and all those questions help the doctor evaluate whether the patient is truly getting the right cardiovascular exercise and how much stress he or she is under–both potential indicators of heart health.

Similarly, a great financial advisor can learn an enormous amount about a client's financial health simply by asking questions about his or her current portfolio. "Why do you have that particular stock?" "What is that fund doing for you?" "Why are you so heavily invested in bonds?" "What is the strategy behind your focus on pharmaceuticals?" "Is there a reason why you don't have significant international holdings?" Such questions will flow spontaneously from one to the next, and the answers provide insights into the client and his or her situation.

Marc Fischer, who was recently named one of *Research Magazine's* 2005 "Top Ranked Advisors in America" and is recognized as a veteran Senior Institutional Consultant at Smith Barney in Rochester, New York, heads a group that advises both institutions and individuals with nearly $750 million in assets under management. "I learn an enormous amount about a client from his or her responses to questions," says Fischer. "Are they intimately involved in their portfolio? Do they understand what is happening? Is there a discipline or process? Is the client comfortable or concerned?"

"Answers to these kinds of questions can vary substantially. At one end of the spectrum is the client with the rationale behind every holding in his portfolio, and who can explain how each interacts with the whole. He understands what's happening, has a process he follows, and is comfortable with it. At the other end of the spectrum, however, is the person who barely remembers when something was purchased and certainly not why. Often, he is not even concerned or interested."

The classic advisor approach involves disturbing or worrying such a client. Great advisors, however, tend to take a different tack. After assessing the situation, they work with the client to pique his or her interest and get the client involved in his or her financial future.

Great Questions to Ask Clients I

A client's or prospect's answers to the following questions will give you insight into who they are and how they truly feel about investing and money:

- How do you make investment decisions?
- Can you recall your earliest memory of money and of investing?
- Do you like to hike or tour alone, or go with a group?
- When investing, do you like to strike out on your own or follow the crowd?
- Growing up, were you rewarded, punished, or loved with money?
- Do you remember the first time you lost serious money—enough money that it affected your lifestyle, plans, or sleep? How did it happen and how did you respond?
- Do you think money can make you happy?
- What does money mean to you?
- What worries you?
- Does anything about money keep you up at night?
- What was your most painful financial mistake? How did you deal with it?
- What was your biggest financial win? How did you feel about it?
- What are you trying to accomplish?
- Is money your first measure of someone's success?
- What is important to you?

When you are probing into a client's money and investment psyche, don't jump to conclusions too quickly. Some advisors are so product-oriented that as soon as they detect the need for a specific product they stop probing and start selling. That can work in the short run. Remember, however, that true financial advice is all about understanding a person's inner feelings, needs, and desires related to money. So it's essential to carefully and completely diagnose the situation before you prescribe the right solution. In the long run, nothing less than this kind of thorough professional approach will work.

Cynthia, a regional executive for a major bank in the Midwest, recounts a classic story. A few years ago, one of the retail bank's investment salespeople met with a bank customer who recently had deposited $400,000 in his checking account. Motivated to close quickly and make the commission, the salesperson pushed his favorite product on the customer. The salesperson was delighted with the quick sale until a month later, when he learned that the $400,000 was pocket change for this person. Worse, within months the customer had pulled his account and gone with an advisor at another firm. When asked why, the former customer said: "The sales guy just blew it. He never took the time to understand my situation. He was too busy closing the sale."

When Cynthia heard about the situation, she was disgusted. "That is not the way we do things around here. Not even close. The bank's approach has always been to slow it down and learn more about the person first. We want to turn customers into clients. The distinction is important. We see customers as people who buy products and services from us. Clients are people who put themselves under our protection. Our mission is to take care of our clients, not just to peddle products and services to customers, and we take that mission very seriously."

Ron, an advisor in Minneapolis, didn't delve deeply enough into his client's reality, either. He quickly concluded that Helen's problem was going to be easy to resolve. At 93 and with no obvious heirs, Helen's only concern–so Ron assumed–was having adequate income for the rest of her life. Helen's assets consisted of a few dollars in the bank, her monthly Social Security checks, a mortgage-free home, and a parcel of developable land worth a little more than $1 million. With the help of a Realtor, Ron worked out a plan that called for Helen to sell the land on an installment plan that would pay her $110,000 a year for 12 years. Ron thought that amount, coupled with her Social Security, was more than adequate to maintain Helen's lifestyle.

But Helen was offended and bluntly turned down the proposal. "What happens after 12 years?" an indignant Helen asked. Her eyes narrowed and lips tightened. "Listen, I know I'm going to die someday, but I'm certainly not going to do it on your schedule!"

Ron thought he had followed a key rule of financial advice: always do the right thing for your client. Yet he ended up offending that client because he diagnosed her situation and prescribed a "treatment plan" without taking the time to fully appreciate her point of view. Once he understood Helen's position, he went back to the drawing board and worked out a plan under which Helen could reinvest part of her income and maintain an adequate cash flow indefinitely. By accounting for her needs and feelings, Ron managed to keep the account.

THE 80-20 RULE

Many advisors talk too much and too soon. Even asking the right questions isn't worth anything without also listening to the answers and then probing deeper. A good target for advisors to strive for in initial client meetings lies in yet another application of the 80-20 rule: Listen 80 percent of the time and then talk the remaining 20 percent. If you're like most people, you won't get close to that ideal, but try to anyway. If you achieve only a 50-50 split of listening and talking, you'll still stand far ahead of the crowd.

Starting a meeting by setting the agenda is important. But it's also essential to lay out that agenda in a way that encourages the client to talk first. When he first started out as an advisor, Bill McIntosh, today a top advisor in Boston, Massachusetts, began his client meetings by saying something like, "I thought what we would do today is talk a little about our firm, its philosophy, and approach. Then we will talk a bit about you. Lastly, we will determine if we should take some next steps. Does that make sense to you?"

The problem with that approach, McIntosh recognized, was that he spent too much time talking about himself and the firm. So, many years ago, he changed his approach to one that concentrated on the client. His opener these days: "I thought we would start by asking you some questions about you, your family, your goals, and your financial experiences. Then I'll tell you a little about our firm, our philosophy, and resources. Then we will discuss what potential next steps we want to take from there." "That approach makes all the difference," McIntosh says.

Don't position yourself to pitch a product. Instead, position yourself as a professional in much the same way a physician does.

Adds Merrill Lynch's Paul McCauley, "When you walk into your doctor's office they don't pitch you. If we want to be perceived as professionals, we must act that same way."

Two Personas

Which tack does the great advisor take?

1. Walks into a room and says, "Look, everyone. Here I am!"
2. Walks into a room and says, "Aha. There you are!"

Answer: Number 2!

Burt was a master listener and a legendary salesman. He didn't like to give speeches, but his company's president leaned on him to share the secret of his success at their upcoming annual meeting. Burt finally agreed. At the meeting he walked to the podium, introduced himself, and then said: "The most important thing I have learned about building relationships is this: only sell to people who buy, and only sell to them when they are ready to buy." He started to walk back to his chair, then, realizing his audience wanted more, he returned to the lectern and added, "And the way you figure that out is to see clients as individuals, ask a lot of questions, and be genuinely interested in their answers." End of speech.

In his brief, blunt speech, Burt told his audience to do a "needs analysis," then sell based on that customer's true need. Translating Burt's advice to the realm of investment advising, success means knowing your clients' and prospects' financial goals, concerns, resources, needs, and objectives. This puts you in a position to advise and serve them to their advantage.

FORGET THE LECTURE

Most clients don't want a prepared lecture or slick PowerPoint presentation. They want to be heard and understood. They want to talk with a caring, intelligent, and well-informed investment expert. Investment advising isn't about entertaining a client or prospect. It's about focusing on the client's needs.

When you're with a client, take your attention off *your* ideas, *your* products, and *your* presentations. Know all the details so well that you can focus on your client. Do more than simply listen to the client's words. Pay attention to and pick up on the unspoken communications, the subtext that lies in a client's face, body language, and tone of voice. Then ask more questions so that the unspoken gets said. As one great advisor puts it: "I listen to my clients with the attention and excitement of a first-time skydiver in a parachute-packing class. I hang on every word, notice every gesture, and ask any question that pops into my head." (More on listening in Chapter 2.)

Phil, an advisor with a major bank on the West Coast, recalls a meeting he had with a prospect that started off on the wrong foot but taught him a valuable lesson. First, Phil resented being present at the meeting. It was Saturday afternoon, and that morning he had coached his son's soccer team to victory. But instead of celebrating with the kids, he had to attend this meeting with a $3 million prospect who had insisted this was the only possible time to meet. The prospect began the meeting by saying he didn't think he needed an advisor, then turned to the banking partner to review a loan application. Phil sat there, he says, thinking to himself, Why am I here? Who does this guy think he is? and This whole thing is a waste of time.

Later, however, driving home, Phil realized his mistake. Instead of thinking about himself at the meeting, he should have been listening to the conversation and focusing on the prospect. It's a mistake, he says, he won't let happen again.

No one will know for sure what Phil might have learned had he paid attention, but the possibilities are endless. After all, a loan application contains an enormous amount of information about a person's financial situation–what they have, what they owe, what they need, and what they are trying to do.

REMOVE EMOTIONS FROM INVESTING

The majority of investment mistakes are not failures of the intellect but are the result of emotional sabotage. And it isn't always conscious emotions that cause the biggest problems; it's the hidden ones. A client may not even realize that he or she is acting on a hidden emotion. That's why the single most important contribution an advisor can make to his or her clients' financial future is often to help them get their emotions out of both their investment plans and the ongoing review process. Advisors can do this by helping their clients bring these emotions out into the open and discuss them.

Another of *Barron's* Top 100 Financial Advisors, John Rafal, is president of Connecticut-based Essex Financial Services, Inc., which provides advice to wealthy families with assets of more than $1.5 billion. Despite his experience and expertise, Rafal couldn't quite figure out why his client, Karen, insisted on an incredibly aggressive approach to investing. She was young, successful, and wealthy, and didn't need to play fast and loose with her investments. Nonetheless, she kept coming up with one weak rationale after another to substantiate her approach. Undaunted, Rafal kept asking questions in hope of getting to the real reasons behind his client's strategy. Finally, he asked Karen about her siblings, and the floodgates opened. Karen's father, it seems, had left her with a considerable inheritance, but he had given his business to her two brothers. They had built it into an empire, and she wanted to get even with them.

Once Rafal understood the underlying reasons for his client's approach–her investment wiring–he was able to help her overcome the emotional aspect of her investing and instead help her put together a wise investment strategy. That level of interest and concern is what every client and prospect has the right to expect from his or her financial advisor.

Ruth, an advisor on Florida's Gulf Coast, talks about a prospect who refused to invest in anything but real estate. "Robin, a single parent in her late 30s, had made a pile of money flipping Florida condos. It's not only that she was convinced that real estate was the only place anyone would make money, she had fallen in love with real estate. Worse, she had come to think of herself as having something of the Midas touch. Being quite a bit older than she, I had been through a few real estate cycles and was concerned because she was rolling over all of her winnings into ever more leveraged projects. Our conversation was going nowhere until I took a chance and asked her if she had ever fallen in love with a man and had him disappoint her. That opened the floodgates so that all I needed to do was make the analogy to the risks of falling in love with an asset class. Then I told her specific stories of clients who had gotten into trouble by overconcentrating in real estate."

Whether a client has fallen in love with a particular financial guru, asset class, stock, or perception of his or her own ability as an investor, the ensuing romantic trance can cloud the client's vision and get the client into a bundle of trouble. Great advisors remove emotions from the investment process.

THE TAKEAWAY

What makes a great financial advisor?

- Knowledge of investment and financial markets
- A client-centric approach to financial advising
- Asking the right questions and truly listening to the client's responses
- A genuine interest in clients' lives
- A passion for becoming an integral part of a client's family fabric
- The ability to identify emotional issues and then help the client remove emotion from the financial decision-making process
- Producing the right results for clients

Chapter

2

WHAT SHOULD YOUR CLIENTS EXPECT FROM YOU?

Not so long ago, financial professionals had a virtual monopoly on investment information. The pros knew, the customers and clients didn't, and the disparity in knowledge was so great that advisors didn't always have to be on the very top of their game.

But the playing field has changed. Thanks to the Internet and television, information has been democratized. Clients and prospects now have access to resources that allow them to be as current as the professionals. In fact, we're all bombarded by so much financial information–valuable and not–that it's become crucial to know which information to use and which to disregard. Adding to the confusion, the financial profession is extremely competitive and crowded with advisors of varying quality.

WHERE'S THE REAL ADVICE?

Most financial professionals believe they take a long-term, client-centric, advice-based approach, but in reality some have a way to go. The title "advisor" can be an important step in the right direction, but it hardly makes someone a qualified expert. How many people do you know who call themselves planners or advisors, yet somehow seem to sell the same product to almost everyone? If all those advisors' clients end up with virtually identical plans, strikingly similar investment allocations, the same mix of money managers, mutual funds, or annuities, or the same basic life policy, chances are that the so-called advisor is driven more by pure product sales than by each client's best interest.

John, an advisor in Atlanta, Georgia, worked hard to obtain all the proper credentials. He was a Certified Financial Planner™ (CFP®) and a Certified Investment Management Analyst (CIMA). One day while at a neighbor's barbecue, he began chatting with someone who handed him a business card that read "Financial Planner." Assuming that the man, like himself, was a qualified professional investment advisor, John started to talk about the investment business. Initially, the man stared blankly at him, and then he began to pitch John to sign up for a multilevel marketing plan to sell soap!

In case you think John's was an isolated case, try searching the Internet for *investment advice.* We googled it and came up with more than 56 million entries. Newspapers, magazines, and the broadcast media probably do a much more responsible job of promulgating investment information, but it's a tragic error when investors confuse such information with advice.

You, as a professional advisor, must work with your clients and prospects to recognize the difference between information and advice. That means telling them like it is: how financial advice and information can be and often are misconstrued, misdirected, or misused.

THE MEDIA'S VERSION

In the 1970s film *Network,* the actor Peter Finch won an Academy Award for his role as a combative newscaster, whose memorable rant to his viewers was that he was "mad as hell and . . . not going to take it anymore."

Fast-forward 30 years. Consider television financial personality Jim Cramer, who, on his daily CNBC show *Mad Money,* shouts his stock market advice to an audience that hangs on his every investment word. CNBC promotes the show as "featuring lively guest interviews, viewer calls, and, most importantly, [sic] the unmatched, fiery opinions of Jim himself."

Unlike some in the financial media, Cramer is not just a talented television host. He's the founder of and market commentator for TheStreet.com. More important, he's also an investment insider who may well be as brilliant as he is outspoken. He seems to care about his viewers' success, evidently knows stocks, and is reported to have established a fine record running a hedge fund. While the man and his show are not to everyone's taste, many viewers find him compelling and entertaining, and his stock opinions valuable.

We have only one concern.

According to the show's Web site. "Jim serves as the viewers' *personal guide* through the confusing jungle of Wall Street investing, navigating through both opportunities and pitfalls. . . ."

What concerns us is the phrase "*personal* guide." How can anyone in the media be a *personal* guide when he or she doesn't know the audience members *personally*? No television host knows the IQs, attitudes, feelings, or emotions of each individual viewer. Hosts don't even know the answers to the most basic data questions that any advisor would need to discover before personally guiding a client, including that client's age and health, income, assets, liabilities, and family and business responsibilities. In fact, unless a person calls in, television show hosts don't even know their viewers' names, and even then, it's first names only.

Cramer sometimes expresses disrespect for financial advisors, yet his show opens with the caveat that viewers should contact their investment advisors before making any decisions on a particular investment. Even the CNBC Web site for the show includes a similar caution: "Securities, financial instruments or strategies mentioned in this show may not be suitable for all investors. This material does not take into account your particular investment objectives, financial situations or needs. . . . You must make your own independent decisions . . ."

These caveats are probably in place because Cramer and his employers realize that he doesn't know his viewers personally and cannot, as a practical matter, offer them financial advice.

The first rule of financial advice is *not* to know about stocks, bonds, mutual funds, insurance, annuities, or markets. Such knowledge is essential, but it's secondary to knowing your client. Not only is that the right thing, it is the law. As anyone who has ever studied for a securities exam knows, the "suitability rule" (Rule 2310) of the National Association of Securities Dealers (NASD) requires that advisors' recommendations for clients are appropriate for their situation. The original intent of suitability rules was to stop brokers from soliciting transactions from everyone and anyone. A broker is required to learn the essential facts regarding every client and every investment he or she offers. In addition, the broker must have a reasonable basis for believing that the investment meets the client's needs and goals and that the client understands and can handle the risk.

As you can see, because of its very nature, the media cannot come close to meeting that first test of knowing the client. The best they can do is know their demographic–the size of the audience and a few of its statistical characteristics. They then can offer generic suggestions and even modify those suggestions to fit broad categories of people and situations. But they can't give universally appropriate advice to individuals they do not know. Part of your job as an advisor is to help your clients understand the limitations of media-driven investing.

The media, however, *are* a crucial source of financial information, news, and commentary that keeps all of us up-to-date. Used appropriately, the media are vital and valuable.

N*ASD* **S***uitability* **R***ule, 2310*

In recommending to a customer the purchase, sale, or exchange of any security, a member shall have reasonable grounds for believing that the recommendation is suitable for such customer upon the basis of the facts, if any, disclosed by such customer as to his other security holdings and as to his financial situation and needs.

Prior to the execution of a transaction recommended to a noninstitutional customer, other than transactions with customers where investments are limited to money market mutual funds, a member shall make reasonable efforts to obtain information concerning:

1. The customer's financial status
2. The customer's tax status
3. The customer's investment objectives
4. Other information used or considered to be reasonable by such member or registered representative in making recommendations to the customer

RECOGNIZE THE DISTORTIONS

In large part, the *investment advice* that financial media pundits pound out really is trading information in the guise of investment advice. If you're a day trader, it might be timely enough to be relevant. For a long-term investor such information is distracting. It may even be dangerous to a long-term investment strategy because it encourages short term behavior.

Some of society's perceptions of the media contribute to this all-too-common distortion of what true investment advice is. Many people often put members of the media on a pedestal, especially those who are old enough to remember when Walter Cronkite anchored the *CBS Evening News* and was, based on numerous polls, "the most trusted person in America." These days, media mogul and talk show host Oprah Winfrey is considered a trusted friend by many.

Yet television personalities are not personal friends with most viewers. Corporations that own the various broadcast and Internet entities aren't charitable institutions, either. As publicly traded companies, most are focused on income, expenses, and earnings per share. Media honchos know that their bottom line comes from advertising revenues, which, in turn, are a function of ratings and circulation.

Fox News Channel CEO Roger Ailes said it well: "Television is not an entertainment medium or a news medium; it's an advertising medium."

In a very real sense, advertisers are the audience that commercial television really cares about. That means the subject matter, stories, and the shows themselves are selected because they draw an audience that advertisers want. In other words, shows are chosen because they are interesting to the public, even if they are not necessarily in the public's interest. The emphasis is on the dramatic and exciting. Put yourself in the media's shoes: which is more exciting to watch, a show that provides meaningful discussions of financial and estate planning issues with careful analysis and in-depth case studies, or one that treats the markets as an ongoing horse race with reports on daily movements and real or imagined causes and concerns?

You get the picture. Make sure your clients and prospects do, too.

GET THE EMOTION OUT

As we mentioned earlier, a good advisor helps his or her clients get the emotion out of their investment decisions. Unfortunately, the information overload that bombards the public serves only to heighten rather than lessen emotions when it comes to investment decisions. Instead of calming fears of inflation or tempering hysteria about the next great bull market or devastating bear market, media reports often exacerbate or inflame such emotions.

Ross Mayer, of Commonwealth Financial Group, who has long been a top investment advisor representative, puts it this way: "The media don't have to live with people's feelings day in and day out. I believe they simply prey on fear and greed. After 37 years in the business, I have met with untold numbers of real people who have lost out as a result of the so-called advice of media talking heads. It fell to me to deal with their emotions and help paste their portfolios back together."

Says Smith Barney's Marc Fischer: "The financial media today do a good job reporting and releasing news and newsworthy stories. However, the media are not accountable as a financial advisor might be. They deliver news which can be incorrectly interpreted as advice by many listeners."

"It's all very frustrating as an investment advisor," says one successful Washington, D.C.–area advisor. "Just the glut of financial news causes a lot of wear and tear on my clients and me. Most investors don't need to know how the market is doing minute by minute, hour by hour, or even day by day. It's of no value to a client with long-term needs and long-term plans. Yet, many people think it is, and it makes them crazy. It often causes clients to think in a manner that is contrary to their best interest."

Her partner adds, "I've heard that doctors have to spend a lot of time explaining away the information their patients get from the Internet and those television ads for prescription drugs. Well, we expend a lot of time and energy doing about the same thing."

Nonetheless, doctors have the right idea. They *do* have a duty to their patients to clear away any misinformation or half-truths picked up from television or the Internet. Investment advisors, too, have a responsibility to explain away the noise! As a personal advisor, you should capitalize on the media's hot-button entertainment approach. Show clients your value, a big chunk of which comes from your professional qualifications and a personalized approach. Don't lose track of the importance of the client-centric mantra as opposed to the transaction-centric one typified by media personalities who push stories of the moment without regard for an individual investor's unique financial needs and goals.

Great advisors help their clients navigate the information overload to find that island of calm, deliberate, unemotional, and rewarding investing. Imagine a television host opening his or her program, "There really isn't much going on in the financial world today. Risk is low and earnings are stable. Why don't you watch a movie or go play with your kids?"

That may sound a bit far-fetched, but it's exactly the kind of tranquil message that professional advisors can and should provide to their clients. They help them turn down the volume, ignore the hubbub, and concentrate on what is really important. Good advisors have the technical knowledge and experience to fight through the maze of information to the essence. They don't dazzle with data, push with products, or manipulate by fear and greed.

We also like to think of great advisors as being emotionally eloquent, that is, possessing the skill and perseverance to persuade their clients to do what they ought to do even when they're not especially inclined to do it. Great advisors are not afraid to take a stand and confront clients with reality. They listen with care, question with intelligence, and confirm with patience. Emotional eloquence leaves no room for a manipulative agenda, but means understanding intellectually, validating emotionally, and then decisively moving to a rational plan of action.

Art is an up-and-coming superstar advisor in Baltimore who attributes a good part of his success to this emotional eloquence. "I am deadly serious about my practice and the value of my contribution to my clients. Throughout my meetings with clients, I work hard to find just the right question to ask so I can get the client on track."

Art recounts an interview he had with a recently retired physician, who, along with his wife, planned an enjoyable–and costly–retirement. The doctor wanted to put his entire $2 million portfolio into bonds, which was far too conservative for him to maintain the lifestyle he and his wife planned. "This fellow was a bit of a know-it-all, and I wasn't getting through," Art says. "Finally I asked him, 'Doctor, how will it feel for you when you have to go back to work?' This clearly got his attention and got us on track."

Shortly before he was about to retire, Ray and his wife, Shirley, met with Ken, an advisor in the St. Louis area, to help plan their retirement finances. Ray, a midlevel corporate executive, had most of his money in a pension account valued at about $1.8 million. All of it was invested in his company's stock.

Ken worked hard to develop a comprehensive plan that focused on protecting the couple's retirement by diversifying their assets. It was coming together until Ray got cold feet. He called Ken and nervously but assertively said, "I've decided to keep all of my money in my company's stock. The company and the stock have been good to me, and I don't want to take any chances."

Ken says he recognized there was no logical way he could persuade Ray to do otherwise. "And I guess I snapped a little bit. I said, 'Ray, do you want me to respond in a professional manner? Or do you want me to tell you how I really feel?'"

After an uncomfortable pause, Ray asked for the truth, and Ken says he laid it on him. "You are out of your [expletive deleted] mind!"

Ken hadn't known it, but Shirley was on the extension, and she chimed in, "You see, Ray. I told you so!" Ken ended up helping Ray and Shirley diversify.

USE PLAIN ENGLISH

Great advisors ditch the jargon, too. Sometimes new investment advisors complicate matters in an effort to impress their clients. Great advisors know better. They forget the buzzwords, and are careful not to overload clients with alphas, betas, Sharpe ratios, information ratios, upside/downside capture ratios, and the like. They take the complexities of investing into account, but then strip away the unnecessary gook. You should do the same.

For example, advisors often approach a client's need for diversification by blending money managers and/or mutual funds in a way that softens the ride under varying market conditions. Technically speaking, that's blending asset classes and money managers' styles so that they have a low correlation to one another. But unless your client is an engineer, mathematician, or physicist, using the latter terminology runs the risk of losing the client's interest or, worse, commitment to the strategy.

One advisor learned that lesson the hard way early in his career while trying to convert a prosperous prospect into his first big client. The advisor thought he had made an impeccable presentation, complete with big words, fancy charts, and precise illustrations. The prospect, however, had other ideas. "Young man," he said, "I may not know much, but I know this: Just because I don't understand something doesn't make it good."

With rare exception, practical speak trumps technical speak. Mike, a successful advisor in the Cleveland area, told us this: "Assume I put together an investment strategy for a nervous client and that it is designed to lessen the impact of market ups and downs. Let's say it involves four money managers, each of whom performs quite differently. When I present the plan to my client, instead of using words like *volatility* and *negative correlation,* I use plain English." Mike went on to say that he prefers words like *up* and *down* and *zigs* and *zags*. For example, he might tell his client, "We have selected these managers because historically when one zigs, the other zags, and that will reduce your risk and help you sleep at night."

Mike goes a step further, too, tailoring his follow-up remarks to the interests of the particular client. If the client is a sports fan, he might also say, "These managers will function as a team in your portfolio. They will play well together for you." Or to a performing arts lover, Mike could say, "These managers will dance well together."

By knowing as much as possible about his clients ahead of time, Mike is able to communicate in a way that relates to them.

If the client accepts the approach, Mike then also cautions the client that this kind of diversification only works if one stays with it and periodically rebalances the portfolio. A common mistake many investors make is that they say they agree with the approach, but when one money manager does well and the other doesn't, they want to pull their funds from the poorly performing manager and give it to the recent winner. The investors forget that the plan was designed to reduce the ups and downs so it could provide performance without heartburn.

"Clients need to be reminded repeatedly of the rationale behind the strategy of using multiple managers," Mike adds.

ASK DEEP QUESTIONS

Talking to clients and asking simple questions isn't enough. To get to a client's or prospect's real feelings toward money and investing requires you as an advisor to dig deeply.

Says one great advisor, "I see myself as a diagnostician who requires all the information possible to do my job. I ask questions, listen to the answers, and probe further. Of course, I want the facts and figures, but I really need the feelings."

Pamela, an advisor in south Florida, built a substantial practice helping retirees with their investment and estate concerns. She credits a visit to her doctor with transforming her practice. "Like most people, I have seen my fair share of preoccupied doctors who treated me as just one more patient. You know the type, the ones who kind of talk to you while they stand impatiently with their hand on the doorknob. Then, I had an appointment with a doctor who became my role model for what an advisor should be. First, he had all the right credentials on his wall. I was impressed, and that motivated me to get serious about completing the course work I needed to get my credentials.

"There was a lot more. He has this simple, yet powerful method for developing a close and thorough understanding of his patient's condition and mental attitude. He starts by asking his patients how they feel, and then he listens to their answers. But he doesn't stop there. He keeps probing further, and he does it by simply asking, 'What else?' He repeats the question over and over, varying the words slightly so it doesn't seem like an interrogation."

Great Questions to Ask Clients II

Among the many ways to ask clients for more information:

- Is there something else?
- Do you want to add anything?
- Is there anything further?
- Is there something more I should know?
- Is there something you are not saying?

Pamela continues, "I asked him why he does it, and he says it is the only way he knows to get a complete picture of a patient's condition and the circumstances surrounding it. I am still amazed at what a difference that simple question 'What else?' has made to my understanding of my clients."

Great advisors do that kind of probing and more. They are willing to take chances in the conversation. They don't interrogate clients and prospects, they interview them. Rather than sell the virtues of a particular product or strategy, they seek information about their client. They are willing to probe more deeply than the client may want to go to get the information they need. They listen their way to a relationship with a client.

UNDERSTAND HOW TO LISTEN

Because we all spend so much of our lives listening, you'd think we would be accomplished listeners. Not so. Eavesdrop on a few conversations at a restaurant, and you'll quickly get the picture. Instead of meaningful dialogue between dinner partners, chances are you'll hear most people engage in a series of monologues, only half-listening and then talking when the other person stops.

Few of us even pay much attention to the subject of listening. Schools offer courses on reading, writing, and speaking, but listening courses are rare. We're bombarded regularly with professionally crafted sound bites that require little effort to hear and further exacerbate our ineptitude at listening. Even technology contributes to dumbing down our listening skills. We crank up our iPods, turn on our cell phones, and stare at our televisions, handhelds, and PCs while the world and the people around us go unnoticed.

Nonetheless, one of the most important descriptions of a great advisor is "someone who listens." In fact, for virtually every advisor we asked, *listening* was at or near the top of their list of essential skills.

Clients have every right to expect their advisors to pay attention to what they say, and to be fully present and alert during the process. After all, advisors must get all the facts and feelings before they diagnose and prescribe. Conversational essentials for this kind of listening and meaningful dialogue include:

- Getting a client to talk to you
- Listening to him or her openly, patiently, and without an agenda
- Probing further whenever needed
- Providing input

For you as an advisor to achieve all this requires more than opening your ears and mind. It's also actively engaging your client or prospect in a serious, deep, and high-level conversation with a full and open exchange of ideas, opinions, and feelings about money.

Value of Questions

What we think of as the moment of discovery is really the discovery of the right question.

Jonas Salk, 20th century scientist credited with discovering the polio vaccine

Questions are the breath of life for a conversation.

James Nathan Miller, author

KNOW THE DETAILS

Let's look more closely at what it takes to truly listen.

Getting a client to talk starts with the listener's attitude. Have you ever met someone and thought "this is a person of few words"–only to have the person turn into a nonstop chatterbox when you got to know each other better? That doesn't happen because of a personality change. It happens because your acquaintance feels differently about your trustworthiness and your interest in him or her.

If, as writer James Nathan Miller put it, questions breathe life into a conversation, then the listener's attitude and reactions are the context that can either energize or suffocate the dialogue. Even in a social situation, the listener is at least as responsible for the quality of the conversation as the speaker is. Think about your own reaction when you're on an airplane, perhaps flying home exhausted from a business trip, when your seatmate suddenly wants to be your new best friend. Most of us don't say, "Buzz off," but we do our best to get that message across, physically. We cringe a little, turn our body away, cross our legs, or get out our laptop. If none of that works, we put on the headset and turn up the sound.

The role of listener takes on even more importance between an advisor and a prospect or client. A speaker takes his or her direction from the listener, Ralph G. Nichols asserts in his classic book *Are You Listening?* (McGraw-Hill, 1957).

All this puts the onus on you, the advisor, to assume full responsibility for a complete and open discussion with your clients and prospects. This doesn't mean you control the dialogue. Trying to do so actually will stifle it. Instead, you must listen in a way that moves the discussion forward. Some suggestions on how to do that include:

- Ask the right questions that dig deeply and provide fruitful responses, and then ask more questions based on those responses

- Talk less
- Receive first and send or talk second whenever possible

When most of us start out in our careers, we have to get up the courage to ask for the order. That changes as we gain experience in this business, and asking for the order becomes second nature. Then the difficult part becomes shutting up and waiting for the answer. Never underestimate the power of the pause. Ask questions, probe, and make a presentation when appropriate, but speak only when it promotes progress, and capitalize on the timing of silence.

Again, as we've emphasized, focus on the client. To listen at a deep level, you must remove the attention from yourself, your ideas, your product, your presentation, and your firm, and put it on your client, where it belongs. When you're spending time with that client, he or she is the only person in the world. Look them in the eyes and convey that.

Powerful Ideas

Every time you meet with a client, make sure you notice the color of his or her eyes. If nothing else, it will force you to look at them and see them.

Nicholas Boothman, author of *How to Connect in Business in 90 Seconds or Less*

"I used to see appointments with prospects as a time to present our firm and our philosophy," says Phil, an advisor in Columbus, Ohio. "Meetings with clients were about going over results and explaining them. Before each meeting I would rush around prepping my presentation. I still prepare, but now part of that preparation is for me to spend at least two or three minutes of quiet time. I calm myself down so I can be there with my client."

To listen well takes this kind of attentive power. You can't waste it focusing attention on yourself, your agenda, your presentation, or your life. You must know your product, your presentation, and yourself so well that you can direct your attention away from all that and focus it on listening to and dialoguing with your clients.

Ask your questions, restate them, confirm them, listen to the answers, and then probe further. Take the great advisor's approach:

- Use questions and follow-ups such as:
  - "So what you're saying is . . . ?"
  - "Let me see if I understand."
  - "How would you feel if circumstances changed?"
- Establish eye contact that engages without being overly intimate
- Mirror the client's body language to create connection
- Nod when appropriate, and murmur comments such as "I see," "Hmmm," "Oh," and "Please say more."
- Adopt a tone that matches your client's mood and message

MORE ON LISTENING

The good news is that humans have listening power to spare. We can hear and understand the spoken word at a much faster rate than people talk. Most of us talk at around 125 words a minute. We can hear and understand at a rate somewhere between 400 and 600 words a minute, perhaps even a great deal more. Whatever the upper limit, we have the advantage of being able to listen three or four times faster than we–or our clients–talk.

For most of us, however, that extra brainpower backfires. Instead of using it to listen, we drift and begin to think about other things. We usually can get away with some of that because of our excess listening capacity. But be careful. If you go too far afield, you'll lose your place and not be able to reconnect with what the client is saying. Be on the lookout for ways you might drift from your meeting, including:

- Trying to rush the process. "When is he going to shut up so I can move the meeting along?"
- Searching for the answer too soon. Concerned that we may not know the answer, many of us start hunting through our mental files for an answer before the client has finished asking the question. We sometimes then end up answering the wrong question.
- Allowing something the client said to arouse your own emotions. It could be a crack about investment advisors being unethical, or the stock market being a glorified casino, or something more personal like an off-color remark or a bigoted comment. While clearly at times you should stand up for your beliefs, as an advisor it's important to hear out the client or prospect.

The best advice: focus!

One advisor recounts the story of a client who said she disliked her own children–all of them. Most of us would have a difficult time staying focused on listening to the client and diagnosing her financial situation after hearing such a blunt statement. Our minds might flood with all kinds of unspoken responses and thoughts so that by the time we tuned back in, the client may have already explained that she really doesn't hate her children but is mad at them because they all moved so far away from home.

Another way we misuse our excess listening power is multitasking. Just as it is irresponsible to drive a car at 65 miles an hour while talking on the telephone, eating a pizza, combing your hair, and shouting at the four kids wrestling in the backseat, multitasking while talking to a client is dangerously distracting, too. Even if your meeting is via the telephone, the client will probably sense when you are reading your e-mail, shuffling your papers, or looking for something on your desk. We used to be able to hear people rattling papers. Now with "mute" buttons as standard operating procedure, we just sense it.

A kind of multitasking that does make sense, however, is taking notes. But be careful here, too. Jotting down a few key facts and observations is fine, but don't take dictation. Instead, expand your notes after the meeting.

What should you do with your extra listening power? Author Ralph Nichols suggests:

- Make an educated guess about where the client might be headed
- Review what has been said so far
- Analyze what has been said
- Listen between the lines of what has been said

But proceed with caution. If you perceive a change in your client's demeanor or conversational direction, focus back on the moment to avoid losing the client.

RECOGNIZE THE UNSPOKEN MESSAGE

Studies indicate that the actual text of a conversation carries only a relatively small portion of a communication. The more meaningful information instead lies in the subtext or underlying message. As an advisor, you pick up that message usually by paying attention to the tone of voice, the pace of speech, the interactions between a married couple, and what their body language says.

Ken, the St. Louis advisor we mentioned earlier, recounts a meeting with a couple he thought was going to be a new client. "The husband was sitting there nodding. He was looking me in the eye and had the tip of the frame of his reading glasses touching his mouth. What I didn't notice until it was too late was that his wife had turned her body away, was shifting her weight and avoiding eye contact. When it comes to bread, half a loaf may be better than none, but half a couple is no client at all."

BEYOND THE FACTS

Chris, an advisor in Toronto, was trained as an accountant, and his father had been an engineer. "So," he explains, "when I started my advisory business I was like the police sergeant in that old TV series *Dragnet*. While I didn't say the words, my whole demeanor made it clear. 'Just the facts, ma'am. Just give me the facts and the figures.' My attitude could have been likened to a doctor who walks into your hospital room, looks at the chart, and walks out. I still need the facts and figures, but I now know that the emotions, behavior, and intentions of the client are more important."

For another advisor, the underlying essence is more important than the surface details. This Denver-based advisor always asks new clients to complete a detailed questionnaire and assemble all their relevant documents before their first client meeting. She wants the information, of course, but she also uses it to make a point. "Some of them proudly hand me a large, well-organized set of files; others reluctantly pass me a few slips of paper. Whatever they give me, I take it, thank them, and then set it on the credenza behind my desk. I look at them and say, 'There will be time for all that later. Right now I want to get to know about you and your family.'"

John, the credentialed advisor mentioned previously who talked about his backyard barbecue experience, recounts a situation in which going beyond the initial information paid off for him. Acting on a strong recommendation for a potential client, John contacted Harry, a successful business owner. Harry seemed nice on the telephone and told John that everything was fine with his existing advisor. But John pressed on anyway. "When it comes to your money and your family's future, is just fine good enough? Doesn't it make sense to get a second opinion?"

Reluctantly Harry agreed, but said that John would have to come to his home. Though that was not his usual practice, John agreed to the house call. After social pleasantries about the friend in common who had made the referral, John reminded Harry and his wife, Helen, that he was there to offer a second opinion. So he asked them to show him what they had been doing with their money. "One glance at their statement," says John, "and I saw it had a lot of dust on it. Nothing had been bought or sold for over three years. As I commented on the lack of activity, I noticed that Helen's face was tense and her arms crossed. I asked her if she had any concerns. It turns out that the advisor was an old friend of her husband who was semiretired and had always taken their business for granted."

John used some of the information to get beyond the facts, and, in the end, he netted Harry and Helen as grateful clients.

STEP BACK

Empathy for a client and his or her situation is important, too. This means setting aside your own point of view and prejudices. Even if you don't agree with something a client or prospect says, stifle your urge to control the conversation. If it's important, you should challenge an off-base remark, but wait until you fully understand what the client meant. Your job as an advisor is not to pass judgment; it's to understand your client's emotional logic and then to assess the impact of that logic on his or her financial future.

Sometimes that means resisting your instincts, too, as Bruce, an advisor in Washington, D.C., found out firsthand. "When I first started as an advisor, if a client or prospect said something I didn't like or wasn't buying what I was saying, instinctively I leaned forward, raised my voice a little, and pressed harder. Now I know better. When it isn't working, I lean back and lighten up. It's still counterintuitive to me. I'm a go-getter, and every cell in my body wants to press harder. But that rarely works, so now I force myself to get lighter and let the client or prospect come to me."

The Power of the Pause

There is one "question" that is suited for virtually any situation. It has an important place in everything from an initial prospecting telephone call to a quarterly review with a longtime client.

The "question" is a well-placed pause. Rather than guessing at the right next question, it often makes sense to pause instead. A silence engages your client or prospect and allows him or her to decide what the next question should be.

Most people are uncomfortable with silences and tend to fill them. Prospects and clients are, but so are most advisors. Instead of filling the blanks, lean back and pause.

Just as the funniest things in life tend to be spontaneous, the most powerful exchanges with clients and prospects are often extemporaneous.

Pauses provide the space for a client's unspoken reality to rise to the surface.

Phyllis, a Los Angeles–area advisor, makes an important distinction when dealing with clients who are illogical or off-base in their ideas or approach. She honors the person but challenges their position. "When a client is really off the mark, I feel I owe it to them to attack their position, but I always try to do it in a way that they know I am honoring them and certainly not attacking them personally."

How does she do that? "It's not so much what I say, but how I say it, and how I feel about it. They may be holding a position that is wrong, but they are not idiots or fools. And if they are taking a foolish position, I talk to them from the point of view of 'fools like us'—never from the point of view of 'fools like you.'"

Remember, good listeners are authentic listeners. They are actively and authentically interested in each client. They don't categorize. Hospitals categorize by condition; car dealers stereotype by the car you drive up in; and society makes snap judgments based on age, gender, race, religion, height, weight, buying habits, and on and on.

It is done in the investment business, too. We lump people together by wealth, risk tolerance, job title, and so on. Classifying clients and prospects can be very useful in helping to understand them, target them with the right products, and tailor the right message. But be careful not to pigeonhole your clients. While retirees tend to downsize, plenty of senior citizens are moving into trophy homes. Men may love football more than women do, but female fans can be just as fanatic, and so on. Generalizations can lead you astray. Listen, and get the full picture.

ESTABLISH TRUST

Jennifer, the Chicago advisor, learned a valuable lesson about client trust during an eye examination. "It was early January and I had made a New Year's resolution to make time for a complete physical. That included a visit to an eye doctor. After looking at my eyes for only a few seconds, the doctor stepped back, smiled, and said enthusiastically, 'You would be an excellent candidate for Lasik surgery.' She then went into a sales pitch for the benefits. She even told me her office would help with the financing.

"I was shocked and said I wasn't interested," Jennifer recounts. "What followed was a cursory eye exam by a cool, uninterested doctor. Driving back to my office, I was sorting out my feelings about what had happened when I passed an out-of-shape jogger who apparently had made a different resolution. He was trying to run, and it looked very painful. I thought to myself, Hey pal, you ought to walk before you run. Then I realized that doctors and advisors ought to diagnose before they prescribe. Ask questions and listen before they recommend. That eye doctor didn't come across as a trusted professional. She seemed like a common peddler."

If a client perceives you as a peddler, he or she is unlikely to trust you. And trust is the stock-in-trade of anyone offering advice. It's the foundation of market economics and the financial services industry, and can enhance or erode your value as perceived by a client. Whether it's a lawyer counseling a client, a coach giving pointers to an athlete, or a financial advisor suggesting an investment plan, the probability of success is much greater if the advice is given within the context of trust.

In financial services particularly, for a working relationship to achieve the desired results, a client must have confidence in his or her advisor's character, ability, and truthfulness. "For many clients, a trusting relationship requires more than factual evidence," says Barbara, an advisor in Phoenix. "These clients tend to base their assessment on subjective and emotional grounds. They weigh such things as personality and community reputation heavily."

The issue of advisor trust is magnified by business scandals. Clients still remember the crimes of executives at former energy giant Enron, once telecommunications leader WorldCom, and the international conglomerate Tyco. They recall the accounting scandals involving Arthur Andersen, well-publicized cases of Wall Street analysts keeping their firms' corporate clients happy by publicly touting stocks they demeaned in private, and even the exposure of self-dealing and preferential treatment by a number of big names in the normally conservative mutual fund industry.

With this kind of backdrop, it's no surprise that clients question whether they can trust an advisor's ability, integrity, or concern for them and their families.

"Developing trust takes time," says Merrill Lynch's Paul McCauley. "That can be an issue when you're trying to establish a new client relationship."

McCauley and McGuirk recount a meeting with a prospect who told them they were among 21 advisors he was considering. "How do I know for sure if I can trust you guys?" the prospect asked.

McGuirk opted to be blunt. "Actually, you don't know. In fact, there is nothing we could say today that would have you walk out of here with complete comfort as to that question."

Their meeting didn't stop there, however. The three continued to talk about trust. McCauley and McGuirk discussed the kinds of clients they have and showed the prospect that many of those clients had needs and assets similar to his. They disclosed their conflicts of interest and talked about how they handle them. They reviewed their open architecture, explaining that it allows them to easily interface with outside money managers and other vendors, as well as their philosophy of focusing on the needs of the client, not the needs of any system, and their conviction never to use a proprietary product when some other product is better for a client. They provided references of other clients, and professionals as well, including CPAs and trust and estate attorneys. With their honesty, openness, and professionalism, they gave the prospect the comfort he needed and deserved. He became a client, and eventually McCauley and McGuirk built trust the only way possible—over time.

WALK YOUR TALK!

Many advisors work hard to create dazzling presentations of all they can do for their clients. But telling clients how good your processes and procedures are and emphasizing all you can do for them isn't enough. The real question is, "Does your process live up to your lofty statements?" When we asked Frank Patzke of FP Financial Services in Schaumburg, Illinois, what he stood for, he said, "I'd like to think my clients say that I am good at what I do, but more importantly that I am honest and trustworthy."

Says another advisor on his value, "I help affluent families avoid blowing themselves up financially." Sounds pretty good. It certainly is different, but does he walk the talk? We put his claim to the test when, coincidentally at a cocktail party in Rhode Island, we met a couple who were his clients. "We've worked with him for years," said the wife, adding, "He has protected us from making some pretty stupid decisions." The husband then elaborated. "During the tech craze, I wanted to pour in more money, but he made us take out a bunch and add it to the account we already had with a value manager. For a year or so I gave him a bad time because I thought we had made a mistake listening to him. It turned out he saved us a fortune. Recently, he persuaded us to reduce our exposure to real estate by selling a rental condo in Boston. Shortly after we closed, the market started heading south." That's an advisor who walks his talk!

PAY ATTENTION TO FAMILY MATTERS

Part of helping clients make the right choices is to understand their family–or families–and its dynamics. That goes for immediate as well as extended and nontraditional families, family members, and partners.

As an advisor, your clients have a right to expect you to be willing to ask the right questions about their families, understand their answers, and dig as deeply as needed. At first, some clients may question why you are prying into their personal lives. If your clients question what you're doing, perhaps you've been too limited in communicating your purpose, value, and role. It's key to make it clear to clients that what might seem like deep, personal background information about them and their families needs to be discussed openly. Think about advisor Dick Sumberg, who takes the viewpoint that in order to do his job, he must be a part of the fabric of his clients' lives. He says up front, "In order to do my job, I need to know more about you and your family, and how you all think and feel about money."

If you do the same thing with your clients, most will come to appreciate how relevant family matters are to their financial game plans.

Remember John Rafal of Essex Financial Services, Inc.? In the previous chapter, we recounted his experience with Karen, who wanted to invest way too aggressively. The reason was not apparent–not, that is, until Rafal learned about her perceived rivalry with her brothers. Family situations can make otherwise rational and successful human beings do irrational and possibly self-destructive things.

South Florida advisor Mel shares a telling tale. "One of my best clients, Sol, who is a widower, called me as soon as he returned from a Caribbean cruise with his two sons, one 43 and the other 40. He wanted to have lunch. I knew something was up because it wasn't like him to call. He was very well off, and his financial plan was in great shape. At lunch he kept playing with his food and trying to make small talk. Finally I said, 'Sol, talk to me. Something is bugging you. What's going on?' He went on to tell me that there was a casino on the cruise and he had done a little gambling with his sons. His older son was very conservative in his approach. He bought a book on how to play blackjack and read it before he started. He set a clear limit on how much he was willing to both lose and win. And he stuck to his plan. The younger son was the exact opposite. He was as careless as he was carefree. 'He played stupidly and didn't seem to care whether he won or lost. Worse, he didn't even consider getting up from the table when he was ahead, and then rode it down until he lost the $2,000 he had. Then he wanted to borrow money from his brother and me.'

"So I asked him whether he thought his younger son had a gambling problem. Sol said he doubted it, adding that his was not a gambling family. 'So what's the concern?' I asked him. 'One could say it was a cruise and he had a little fun. So what?'

"Sol replied, 'You know so what. It's his lack of respect for money and his lack of discipline.'"

The issue for Sol, Mel points out, was his will. "Sol's concern was for me to help him figure out a way to keep his younger son from burning through his inheritance without hurting his feelings. That led us to a long philosophical discussion of the pluses and minuses of treating the boys differently. Then we scheduled a joint meeting with Sol's trust and estate lawyer to review and analyze his options."

Heather Walsh offers another perspective on family matters. She's a member of WDC & Associates, a four-person, top-flight advisory team at Merrill Lynch in Burlington, Massachusetts, that has more than $700 million in assets under management. "These days I find that an increasing percentage of my female clients run their money separately from their husband's. I'm not sure why this is happening. Some are dealing with a second marriage, others just married late, and a good number have money they inherited. One couple we work with is in their 80s and have been married quite a while. Yet, they insist we call them on different phone lines to talk about their separate money. You just can't assume when a couple walks into your office that they think of their money as being in the same bucket. The traditional view of family finances that most of us grew up with isn't necessarily the case anymore."

THE TAKEAWAY

- Understand your clients both broadly and deeply
- Listen. Listen. Listen to your clients
- Embrace silences
- Stay with your clients instead of allowing your mind to move ahead or wander
- Diagnose thoroughly before prescribing
- Turn down the media noise for your clients
- Keep your clients focused on what is important
- Wring the emotion out of investment decisions and keep it out
- Dig into family matters
- Confront clients' underlying feelings and concerns
- Don't make assumptions; ask questions instead
- Use plain English
- Tell your clients what you really think
- Take a stand

Chapter

3

CAN YOU RECOGNIZE A CLIENT'S INVESTMENT WIRING?

Each of us have preset inner attitudes, feelings, and biases when it comes to money. We call that our *investment wiring*. Often, it's the result of upbringing and past experiences–good and bad–that impact our attitudes toward money. In many cases we don't even realize it exists. But our investment wiring–steeped in our emotions and often hidden behind a personality façade–can subconsciously or consciously threaten to derail even the best plan to achieve our financial goals.

Imagine an acrobat who doesn't know he or she is atop a high wire. This is the kind of precarious position investors face if they don't understand their own investment wiring. That's because, as we've discussed previously, it's essential to get the emotions out of investment decision making. Those advisors adept at getting beyond a prospect's or client's personality façade–and then identifying, diagnosing, and accounting for investment wiring–stand head and shoulders above the competition. Let's take a closer look at ways to work with a client's investment wiring.

INVESTMENT WIRING UP CLOSE

Put another way, investment wiring is that emotional baggage involving money that we all carry around. It's a combination of usually irrelevant or obsolete beliefs, attitudes, and prior experiences that impede our freedom of thought and actions regarding money, limit our investment progress, and can destroy our ability to reach our financial goals.

Think about Karen, John Rafal's client mentioned previously, who sought to pursue careless, aggressive investing as a way to subconsciously compete with her wealthier brothers. Her reckless investment stance revealed much about her investment wiring and emotional baggage. As Rafal's discussions with her ultimately revealed, Karen was unknowingly basing investment decisions on latent sibling rivalry and, perhaps, a desire to show her father how wrong he had been to cut her out of the family business.

Other types of deep-seated emotional baggage include self-image, family influences, and outmoded theories, notions, and practices. The many elderly people who lived through the Great Depression and insist on buying government bonds and keeping money in federally insured accounts as a hedge in case disaster befalls the economy are prime examples of people falling prey to their intellectual and emotional baggage. It doesn't matter that their accounts don't even keep pace with the rate of inflation, let alone meet their long-term goals. Logic and fact are unlikely to prevail when dealing with this kind of emotion-laden investment wiring.

Faulty investment wiring can be compared to electrical wiring. If a circuit breaker cuts off the power, all you do is flip the central circuit breaker and the power comes back on. If it continues to go off, you call in an electrician to uncover the underlying problem. After all, the circuit breaker is a release valve if the current jumps above a safe level. Financial advisors have a similar function. Part of their job is to uncover a client's underlying issues and release the pressure before those issues become a barrier to creating or sustaining a rational investment plan.

Walt, an advisor in Portland, Maine, paints the even bigger baggage picture that advisors usually encounter. "It's not just that one client is carrying a load of baggage. It's that two or more people are each weighed down with their own baggage because, in most cases, you're advising a husband and wife. It gets even more complicated with wealthy families, where you're often dealing with multiple generations, splintered families, differing charitable objectives, and so on. And let me tell you, that baggage is rarely a matching set!"

GETTING BEYOND THE FAÇADE

The biggest obstacle to identifying a client's or prospect's investment wiring often is the façade they've spent years perfecting. In plain–if somewhat crude–English, you must learn how to overcome their façade, the persona they've adopted to blow you off. Advisors are familiar with the routine: you meet a new prospect or client who, in the first few encounters, reveals more and more of a certain type of personality, whether penny-pinching, cynical, know-it-all–you name it.

Take Mel and his client Sol, whom we talked about in the past chapter. When they first met 25 years earlier, Sol was the ultimate cynic and a real pain. He still operated his business in a tough neighborhood in New York City and saw the world as peopled with chiselers. His biting personality, however, was a façade that hid his investment wiring, his deep-seated baggage. While the underlying causes vary from person to person, Sol's case was rooted in the way he had inherited the family business years earlier. Keeping with traditional views, his father had left his entire business to Sol with the provision that Sol provide an income to his two sisters. The problem was that the business was hurting, and his father's lawyer and accountant had done a lousy job of estimating its value. Sol not only had to rebuild the business from less than zero, he had to deal with his sisters' ire, too. They were convinced he was cheating them, and one even sued her brother. No wonder Sol had grown bitter and cynical. It took Mel years to understand Sol. But once he did, Sol's cynical personality evaporated—at least around Mel.

Unfortunately, many advisors can't or won't spend the time to get beyond the personality façade. They never understand a client's deep feelings toward money and, in turn, fail to prescribe the right financial regimen. For example, when we asked Troy, a young advisor from the Detroit, Michigan area, about the role of identifying a client's investment wiring, his response was, "It can't be done. They won't tell you that stuff. All you can do is power past them and get them to buy something. Then maybe later you can get to know them."

Too bad Troy wasn't willing to dig a little deeper. Not only would he have found that he was better able to serve his clients and provide them with more of his firm's services, but he would have discovered that his own retention numbers were improving as well. After all, as we mentioned earlier, studies repeatedly show that the more of a firm's services a client uses, the more likely that person is to remain a client.

Identifying and dealing with a personality early also can improve your closing ratios. You won't waste as much of your time on dead-end prospects because you'll recognize them quickly. You'll be able to identify "drop-dead" issues, before they get complicated and masked by a maze of facts and figures. Drop-dead issues are those that are unlikely to go away and ultimately can destroy a sale, a financial plan, or an advisory relationship. For example, if a husband brings you in for an interview and it turns out that the couple's existing advisor is his wife's cousin, chances are you're facing a drop-dead issue.

Get these and other emotionally laden issues between a husband and wife on the table early, says Pamela, the south Florida advisor. Her approach: "I'm not here to cause trouble in your relationship. Before we go any further, please tell me what the chance is that you can come to an agreement to make a change?"

Smoking out similar drop-dead issues and dead-end prospects early improves your closing ratios in two ways. First, it saves you time by allowing you to move on to more fruitful prospects. Second, it may help you handle an issue that, if left to fester, could cause problems later on in the process.

Another benefit of dealing with these issues early is that it may help you to move beyond a prospect's or client's personality straight to his or her investment wiring. For example, with Pamela and the couple previously mentioned, the wife's underlying issue may have been related to trust or comfort levels. The husband, on the other hand, might be wired to be more of a player at investing. In that case, it's likely he's grown impatient with what he sees as a comfortable relationship but second-rate performance. Pamela, therefore, has to deal not only with the relationship with the wife's cousin, but also with the husband's and wife's unmatched set of baggage. Of course, this is just one possible scenario of what might be the couple's underlying baggage.

When a prospect or client comes across as a particular personality, recognize it, acknowledge it, and deal with it. If you don't, it can come back to haunt you. Think of that personality as a barrier you must break through to do your job. You get beyond the barrier by asking the right questions and engaging in the right kind of dialogue.

The head of sales for a successful investment sales organization offers this assessment: "If you identify a control freak early, you can call them on their attitude up front. If you can get through to them, great. Go on. But if you can't, there is no point in using your sales skills to get an appointment or build a plan, only to have their personality rear its head and stop you cold later in the process. You can avoid wasting a lot of time and energy if you confront the issue head-on when it first comes up."

FAMILIAR PERSONALITIES

When you're trying to break through a personality façade to get to a prospect's or client's investment wiring, it's helpful to quickly identify his or her general personality type. A few classics include:

- Mr. Cocky or Mr. Know-It-All, who thinks he's smarter than you and has all the answers about money, investments, and just about everything else
- The Cynic, who questions everything you say and believes that you are interested only in your fees or commissions, not in him
- The Putterer, who, with little else to do, invests to avoid boredom. If he's rich enough, he buys a sports team; if not, he hangs around the lobby of a discount broker.
- The Hobbyist, who sees investing as an expression of personal accomplishment. He's often passionate about investing but rarely professional.
- Paul Perfect, who assures you that his investments and planning are all in fine shape and that he doesn't need your help
- Amy Amiable, who wants everyone to get along. She is easy to talk with but almost impossible to call to action.
- The Analytic, who wants to break down everything you propose to its component parts and examine each one to death, and then doesn't get the overall picture–though he often thinks he does
- The Controller, who insists on setting the agenda and often likes to put you down in the process
- Ms. Pennywise, who is unwilling to pay your fees–or anyone else's, for that matter

While all these caricatures will seem familiar to experienced advisors, keep in mind that they all are generalizations. It's important not to lose sight of the fact that people are individuals and each of their situations is different. Also, personality types often overlap. A Cynic may come across as Pennywise. Controllers often will appear Cocky, and so on. It's also important to recognize that certain behaviors can pop up when you're dealing with any personality type. Chief among those behaviors is procrastination.

Cynics do it; so do Controllers, Analytics, Ms. Pennywise, Paul Perfect, Mr. Cocky, and especially Amy Amiable. Recognizing various personality types is a valuable if imperfect tool to help you deal more effectively with procrastination as well as other debilitating behaviors that may surface.

MR. COCKY, AKA MR. KNOW-IT-ALL

Have you ever heard the line, "I'm better at this than you so-called professionals!"? Meet Mr./Ms. Cocky, aka Mr./Ms. Know-It-All. Confront him/her head-on. Otherwise, whether this persona is a façade or the real McCoy, you and your proposals are likely going nowhere.

Beyond the Words

Ask tough questions, but beware of the subtext—-that underlying message conveyed by tone, inflection, body language, and more. When talking with clients or prospects, make sure your subtext honors their dignity. You are there to help them, you're on their side, and you respect their opinions.

The only thing worse than not selling a know-it-all is making him or her your client, says Stan, an advisor in Orange County, California. "When I first started my career, this young, condescending urologist said to me, 'If I had the time, I could do this better than people like you and all of you so-called experts. But I save lives, so I have to rely on people like you.' How dare he? I should have called him on it and asked him what he meant by 'people like me' or, better, asked him if he had had a bad experience with another advisor. But I was so eager for the business I just kept selling and somehow managed to make him a client. His investments did fine, but for three years he never failed to find a way to demean me. By the time I stood up to him, it was too late.

He went elsewhere, probably to abuse someone else. Part of me says 'good riddance,' but another part of me still believes I could have made him a good client if I had only called him on his behavior sooner."

Now, Stan says, when he recognizes a know-it-all, he tests the client's bravado first, and then, if necessary, calls him on it. "I do my best to resist the temptation to come off cocky myself, and instead start the conversation with something open-ended: 'Really? That's terrific! Tell me more.' If the prospect keeps going on and on about how great he is, I get more specific and ask, 'What's your performance record over the past five years?'"

Mr. Cocky likely won't be able to quantify his returns other than with a general comment. That's OK for the moment. Don't argue. Compliment his success, keep pressing, and overlook his claim that he makes money when he manages it compared with losing money when others manage it. Forget his references to all advisors as "so-called professionals," too. Just move on with the conversation. Mr. Cocky is, after all, seeking your advice, whether simply as validation of his skills or for some other reason.

Most likely, he's not as good a money manager as he thinks he is. That's because investors, especially do-it-yourselfers, tend to forget their losses and remember the winners. They also usually fail to evaluate their entire portfolio. For example, Mr. Cocky claims he gets a 10 percent return on his money—conveniently leaving out the fact that half of his money is in the bank earning considerably less. His real return is a lot lower than he thinks.

Do, however, consider whether Mr. Cocky is really so cocksure or, perhaps, the ultimate cynic or even extremely insecure instead. (More on this later in this chapter.)

Don't debate him. Instead, ask the right questions to help you get through the façade and start building that all-important relationship. A few pertinent questions include:

- Do you have a disciplined and consistent investment process that can be repeated over time? Investing is a long-term proposition. Short-term success often is the result of doing just the right thing at precisely the right time. It's difficult to reproduce consistently.

- Are you lucky as an investor? A big short-term win is exciting and fun, but it's also dangerous. It often creates the desire to repeat it and, coupled with overconfidence, can lead to inappropriate risk taking and catastrophic results. Many investors who scored big in the tech boom in 1999 ended up losing even more a year or two later!
- Do you have a risk-management strategy? Have you developed ways to systematically pare back winners and stop losers, or do you just let them run? When you buy different investments, do you consider how they might interact with each other in terms of risk? Do you allow yourself to become too concentrated in an industry or sector?
- How do you do in tough markets? Because bear markets can be humbling, you're more likely to run into Mr. Cocky in a bull market. When you do, keep in mind how Harvard economist John Kenneth Galbraith defined financial genius: "a rising market and a short memory." Give Mr. Cocky a few years and a bull market, and he thinks he knows it all. So ask how he did in the past bear market.
- When do you decide to sell a stock or a mutual fund? Do you decide on a target when you buy, or do you wait for inspiration later? How do you make that decision?
- Are you better at taking a gain or accepting a loss? Many investors find it difficult to sell whether they're ahead or behind. When things are going up, they think they'll go up forever, and when they're going down, they want to get even, so they hold on.
- Are you a patient or an impatient investor? Do you think it's important for an investor to be patient? How much time do you give an idea to work before you move on? Mr. Cocky likely is impatient. Quick wins satisfy his ego, while losses damage it, and waiting seems a waste of time.
- Do you give your own ideas more time to work than those of others? If so, why? This line of questioning likely will re-

veal how Mr. Cocky's ego gets in the way of his developing and sustaining a rational investment plan. He almost certainly will give his ideas more time than yours. It's an ego thing.
- If you could choose a money manager from among ten people–nine of the best professional money managers in the industry and you–would you pick yourself? Would anyone else pick you? Even the most arrogant incarnation of Mr. Cocky would have trouble with that one.

THE CYNIC

"You people are all the same. You're just trying to sell me something." Sound familiar? Whether said aloud or merely thought, those are the words of the Cynic. Some more familiar refrains include:

- "You're all biased toward the products you and your firm want to sell me!"
- "You don't give a damn about me."
- "You're in the business to fund your corporate clients by peddling their deals to people like me. You don't care if the investments are good or not."

Welcome to the world of the Cynic. Cynics tend to believe that all human conduct is motivated by self-interest. They expect nothing but the worst when dealing with others, so it's easy to see why their outlook usually is scornful and negative. They see little but tough lessons in the past and are disappointed by what's ahead even before it happens.

If you end up dealing with someone who is a committed long-term cynic, you may not want that person as a client. But true cynics are rare, and chances are the Cynic across the desk from you converted to cynicism for a reason. Perhaps you're dealing with a disappointed investing idealist who naively got involved in an investment scheme that went bust. Maybe he was burned by an unqualified advisor. Or maybe he has simply suffered the costly investment consequences of bad timing. Whatever the individual case, you need to discover the person behind the persona or move on.

The Right Side of the Table

The essence of having a constructive, positive influence on another is the ability to form an alliance with them in which the teacher, physician, or advisor is in fact perceived to be the advocate of their student, patient, or client.

Hilliard Jason, MD, EdD, world leader in enhancing and humanizing teaching and communications process in health professions

Some cynics openly make it clear they don't trust you. Others are more covert about their distrust. Watch for clues, and ask questions, including:

- Who do you trust? Your accountant? Your doctor? If the cynic doesn't trust any other advisors, chances are he or she won't trust you, either. If he does trust some professionals and not others, ask why. What is it about that person or that relationship that lends itself to trust? Perhaps it's the longevity of relationship, the method of compensation, or their advisor's credentials. Remember, though, trust is the foundation of any worthwhile advisory relationship.
- Did you have a bad experience with an advisor in the past? If so, how did you select that advisor? Could our experience be different? In what way?
- Is there anything I can say or do to allay your concerns?
- When it comes to working with advisors, do you consider yourself a realist, a cynic, or something else?
- What happened to make you so cynical?

If all else fails, keep in mind that you probably don't want an unbridled cynic as a client anyway.

Remember the openly distrustful prospect in the last chapter who interviewed the team of McCauley and McGuirk as one of 21 different advisors he was considering? His distrust was blazingly clear up front when he asked, "How do I know I can trust you?"

Often, though, the clues pointing to distrust don't announce themselves unless you pay close attention. Kathy, an advisor in San Francisco, does that by focusing on her clients' tone of voice and facial expressions. "Most cynics I've met are dissatisfied with just about everything–and it shows. They are the opposite of an energetic person who has a bright expression on their face, a firm handshake, and who welcomes you with enthusiasm. The Cynic usually isn't glad to meet yet another person who will let them down, so they tend to move slowly, shake hands unenthusiastically, and vaguely glance at you rather than make eye contact. Their facial expressions, body language, and tone of voice are just a little bit sour.

"Some of them come off kind of cocky. Others seem kind of depressed. When I meet them, I start off being my bright cheery self. After all, there is always the chance they are just tired or having a bad day. When that doesn't snap them out of it, I can pretty much assume I have a cynic on my hands. The most successful advisor in our office says life is too short to deal with cynics. But I like to see if I can break through, so I ask a few questions."

Alex, an advisor in Chicago, offers this advice: "My town has its fair share of cynics. Some of them are so good at it, they can get you questioning yourself. Once I sense I'm dealing with one, the first thing I do is remind myself what a valuable contribution I make. I don't want their doubts to get me doubting myself. I review my own value proposition in my head, and then I confront them with it. I am no more a peddler than a doctor or dentist who recommends a course of treatment."

Make sure that the value you bring to your client and how you convey it is clear and powerful enough to silence the toughest critic. If it doesn't, move on.

THE PUTTERER

Investing is prime-time entertainment or a major social event for the Putterer. If he's retired, puttering also is a way to stay connected to the world of business. Who doesn't know a retiree who hangs around the ticker at the local brokerage, calls daily for market updates, or watches CNBC several hours a day?

"If I didn't manage my money, what would I do with my time?" is the Putterer's familiar refrain–that's if the Putterer is honest about it. Some may kid you and themselves by saying, "I have to keep a constant eye on my money. You never know what could happen."

Why do people from unrelated careers think that retirement suddenly transforms them into money managers? Perhaps it's because, without their steady earned income, money takes on new significance. Or maybe they feel that expertise in their past profession magically transfers to the world of investing. Whatever the reasons, many Putterers find out the hard way they're not up to the task. Curing boredom by investing can be misdirected and expensive.

Can you imagine a recent retiree with no professional medical background who, to keep busy, opts to take care of all her medical needs by reading medical journals and googling her condition on the Internet? Chances are the retiree's health would be at risk and her judgment in doubt.

It's the same when it comes to investing. If someone has money to burn and wants to putter with a small amount, that's fine. On the other hand, if prospects or clients are at risk of outliving their money, they need to find a less expensive sport. Even going to a casino and throwing a little money in a slot machine would be a better idea.

A few questions to consider asking the Putterer include:

- Wouldn't you rather be doing something else?
- Do you ever go to a casino? If the answer is, "Yes, but not to gamble," ask why not. Chances are the answer will be some-

thing about the odds being stacked against him or her. If it is, you might say something about the odds being stacked against an individual investor who goes it alone. If the Putterer does gamble, ask "Would you like to have more favorable odds?" Whether or not the Putterer gambles, you'll be in a position to discuss the advantage of using professional help to improve investing odds.

- Would you hire a money manager who says the reason he or she manages your money is to keep busy?
- Doesn't your financial future deserve more? Doesn't it deserve professional help?

THE HOBBYIST

Hobbyists enjoy investing. Their typical line includes: "It's my passion. I savor the intellectual challenge and the emotional stimulation of picking stocks. Watching them go up is a rush."

Often, you can spot a Hobbyist just by glancing at his or her portfolio. Chances are you'll see a lot of positions, many dating back years. If they invest in individual stocks, they likely will be all over the place. If they invest in mutual funds, the list will include many familiar families and funds. When visiting a Hobbyist at home, don't be surprised if he or she is watching a financial news show when you arrive and if financial magazines are stacked in the corners. Hobbyists also probably will say they don't need or want your services. But they're eager for advice on the markets, a stock, or an industry. Once they get that advice, however, don't expect them to place an order through you just because they like what they hear.

The Hobbyist is a close cousin to the Putterer, but with some distinct differences. Hobbyists throw themselves into investing almost as an obsession, compared with the Putterer, whose investing is a way to socialize or keep busy. Think of investing as gardening. The Putterer plants a few plants, tosses out some seeds, periodically waters and weeds, and chats with neighbors.

The Hobbyist, on the other hand, builds a special fenced area, methodically plants it, waters carefully, and weeds every day. Hobbyists also spend a fortune buying all the gardening gadgets, and at night they read gardening magazines.

You get the picture. In much the same vein, Putterers buy a few investments, play at trading, and sometimes overtrade. They may subscribe to the *Wall Street Journal,* but tend to read only those articles that happen to strike their interest. While Putterers might hang around a discount broker's office, they do so because it's a place to go, not because it's a way to stay on top of the investing world. Investing is a game, an amusement, for Putterers.

Hobbyists, on the other hand, buy the best computers, subscribe to an online information service, watch financial news shows, and read *Barron's, The Wall Street Journal, Investor's Business Daily,* and the *Financial Times*. They bore their friends and family with investment stories. Often Hobbyists hang on to their investment positions, sometimes forever, because Hobbyists tend to fall in love with their investments, their money garden.

Your question for the Hobbyist might be whether his or her garden will yield as abundant and healthy a crop as one designed and managed by a professional.

"When this cardiologist showed me his portfolio, I couldn't believe it. It looked like a stamp collection," says Hank, an advisor in Chapel Hill, North Carolina. "The guy loved picking and following funds, and then showing them off. Most people are reluctant to show you what they have. This guy was eager. He owned 44 funds and had his portfolio all organized in a beautiful spreadsheet on his computer. He told me he updated their values once a week. He was in love with them. So I asked how often he sold a fund and he proudly replied, 'Never!'"

Never? Investing is not collecting! Of course, there are some very successful investors who tend to buy and hold, Warren Buffett among them. Says billionaire Buffett, "Only buy something that you would be perfectly happy to hold if the market shut down for ten years."

But Buffett is no hobbyist, and he doesn't buy or hold based on emotion. Investing is his life, and he doesn't play around. Buffett stands ready to become actively involved with a company if things don't go the way he thinks they should. It seems safe to assume that most hobbyists, even if they were smart enough to do it, aren't big enough to step in and take over.

One reason hobbyists are reluctant to sell is that they often become emotionally attached to their positions. Larry, an advisor from Silver Springs, Maryland, talks about a prospect who did just that. After a dinner meeting, she told him, "You know, I really love picking stocks, and I'm good at it. In fact, I bought Google for my IRA rollover right after it came out. I wouldn't buy it today at this price, though!"

So, Larry says, he asked her if she had sold it yet. The response, of course, was, "No way!" "So I asked her what the difference was between holding it and buying it. Wasn't she, in effect, buying it every day she didn't sell it? She glanced at me with a look people usually reserve for a benevolent idiot. Then I said, 'You are an emotional investor, aren't you?' and suggested we talk about it in a follow-up meeting."

One approach to help counter the Hobbyist's unreasoned zeal is to ask him or her to prioritize the following based on level of enjoyment:

- Being with his or her children
- Playing with grandchildren
- Going out to dinner with a spouse or significant other
- Party time with friends
- Going to the theater or seeing a movie
- Playing tennis, golf, or another favorite sport
- Gardening or other outdoor activity
- Running, working out at the gym, or other athletic activity
- Reading
- Investing his or her money

Investing probably would not come out on top. If it does, take another tack like the one suggested by John, the Atlanta advisor in Chapter 2. He compares investing with golf. On a bad day of golf, you could have a few tee shots go out of bounds, miss some easy putts, and perhaps lose half a dozen balls. Aside from losing a bet in your foursome, the ramifications are few, and you'll probably be back on the course the next week. By comparison, a bad year in the markets can mean huge financial losses with no one to blame but yourself. A round of investing like that is certainly no fun and carries plenty of risk.

Another good question for the Hobbyist: which do you enjoy more, managing your investments or making money?

If a client or prospect actually does enjoy the process more than the result, remind him or her that managing investments means both buying and selling. Perhaps, as with the Putterer, one solution is compromise. The Hobbyist can manage a portion of his or her assets, but the majority would be handled by you, the professional. After all, if, in that serious golf game, you had the option of hitting a tee shot yourself or letting golfing great Tiger Woods do it for you, which would you pick? OK, maybe that feels a little like cheating. So, how about Tiger coaching you through the round? Thought so. Go get 'em, Tiger!

As an added bonus of a compromise, delegating the serious money to the pros allows the Hobbyist to avoid some of the must-produce pressure and enjoy investing all the more. Refer to the Hobbyist's share as play money and the greater balance as the serious money on which to build a financial plan.

Geoff, an advisor in western Pennsylvania, uses a somewhat different approach. "A lot of my clients are entrepreneurs and businesspeople. Many of them were really into investing during the late 1990s. When the tech boom went bust, one of my clients invited me to go hunting. He told me the bust had made him realize that all of his money deserved a full-time professional 'steering the ship and adjusting for changes in the weather.' Yet he still wanted a role. I asked him what he thought our respective roles should be. There was a long pause as he thought and I waited. He laid out the simple plan on which I now base much of my business. 'I'll be the CEO in charge of the big picture—the overarching goals and the like. You be the CFO and decide the strategy and tactics. It'll be your job to make it happen.'" Now, that arrangement is working well for Geoff with many of his other clients.

PAUL PERFECT

The new prospect bounces into your office and asserts, "Everything is great. I don't even know why I'm here. I am all set." Chances are if that's the message, you're face-to-face with Paul Perfect.

John Rafal, who we mentioned earlier, has met more than his fair share of this personality type. "When working with Paul Perfect," says Rafal, "your objective should be simple: become part of his perfection. If you do, he is likely to become one of your most loyal clients and most passionate referrers. He likes to brag, and you want him bragging about you. But you can't get there by directly confronting the absurdity of his views. He has to come to his own conclusions."

When Paul Perfect walks into your office, he'll talk about how wonderful everything is, including his investments. You'll then wonder, If everything is so darn great, why is he here? Does he want confirmation of his perfection? If you opt to be blunt and ask, "If things are so perfect, why in the world did you make this appointment?" don't be surprised if he takes it as an attack on his ego.

"Rather than confront him," says Rafal, "I get him to talk by asking questions. I usually start with something of a background nature, perhaps something about his business or career."

- For entrepreneurs, the question could be: Tell me, how did you built your business?
- For doctors: How did you establish your practice?

- With a corporate executive: How did you climb the corporate ladder?
- If the client has a family: Tell me about your family.

When clients appear to be headed in the wrong direction, many of us make the mistake of trying to stop them and set them straight. But Rafal knows better. If a client wants to brag and talk about how perfect everything is, he not only lets them, he helps them and gets them talking. "I've found that if I start by challenging their assumptions, they can go on forever proving how perfect things are. But if I encourage them to talk more, they pretty quickly run out of things to say. Then I can move on to questions of money and planning."

Rafal tends to move to estate-planning issues first and often finds that the client is not as certain about this aspect of his or her financial affairs. "A recent prospect went on and on about how renowned his estate-planning attorney was and how his insurance agent flew in by helicopter to see him. So, I asked him when was the last time he discussed his insurance, trusts, or will with them. It turned out he had not seen the attorney in over ten years and the helicopter in six. Obviously, things weren't so perfect. So, we then were able to move on to discuss his investments and found evidence of similar neglect. There was a sharp difference between perception and reality. His advisory relationships were mythical, and he started to see that."

Rafal then asked more questions to help the prospect along:

- Where are your various advisors falling down on the job?
- What aren't they doing for you?
- Are they doing anything that you feel is unsatisfactory?
- Are they doing anything that is less than perfect?
- Is there anything someone else might do better?

The bottom line in dealing with Paul Perfect is to proceed in increments. Go slowly, encourage him to talk, gradually help him peel back the layers, and let him come to his own conclusions. If you get him as a client and serve him well, chances are you and your business will have the perfect advocate.

AMY AMIABLE

It's only Tuesday afternoon, and already you're emotionally exhausted. On Monday, Mr. Cocky spent two hours telling you he is smarter than you are. That afternoon a surly Cynic sneered at every suggestion you made. Last night, the Putterer hemmed and hawed and wasted your time. This morning Mr. Hobbyist picked your brain, got some ideas, then walked out of your office and called his discount broker from your reception area. After lunch, Paul Perfect puffed up his chest and bragged for 45 minutes about his well-rounded portfolio.

And in walks Amy Amiable. What a relief! She is so nice. You feel like you are meeting an old friend. There's nothing contentious or offensive about her. She is good-natured and well intentioned. Her heart and her wiring are an open book. Getting close to her will be no problem at all. And her husband, Alec Amiable? You are going to like him, too. No doubt working with this couple will be a joy.

The question, however, is will it be productive for any of you? Amy and Alec are likely to have a difficult time making decisions, taking stands, and confronting emotionally difficult tasks, including letting go of an old advisor who isn't doing the job.

Lou, an advisor in Philadelphia, told us about a couple who started off as a dream prospect but proved to be something else entirely. "Initially, Larry and Rose seemed like a star prospect, but they ended up being impossible to budge from the top of my prospect pipeline onto my client roster. Usually, I insist on meeting at my office, but after our initial meeting, they invited me to continue our conversation at their home. It wasn't far and I really enjoyed them, so I went. We had a series of six meetings at their home. Their house was as welcoming as they were. The colors were warm, and the furniture was cozy and comfortable. They always treated me like an old friend of the family. They offered coffee and fresh muffins when we met in the morning, a nice salad if it suddenly became lunchtime, and once a glass of wine in the afternoon.

"Early on they made it clear that they were unhappy with their portfolio's progress. They felt their current advisor was a bit over the hill and wasn't giving them the service he should. Taking the hint, I worked hard to show them how I could and would do a significantly better job. They loved my presentation and even went so far as to sign the papers necessary to move the account. The next morning, Larry called and asked me not to process the papers for a little while. He and Rose wanted some time to break the news to their old advisor and would let me know when they had. They didn't want to hurt his feelings. A few weeks later, Rose called to say Larry was in the hospital and it was serious. I was genuinely concerned and called her three or four times a week to see how he was doing and how she was coping with the strain.

"Now it is eight months later. Larry is out of the rehab hospital and well on his way to recovery. We are still friendly, but Larry and Rose are not my clients. I doubt they ever will be. At least not anytime soon."

Whether their names are Larry and Rose or Amy and Alec, amiable people make great friends. As advisory prospects, however, they can be a drain on your time, your energy, and your spirit. Chances are you'll really like these people, and they'll like you. Therein lies the problem. They like virtually everyone and want to offend no one. Not only will they drag their feet on naming you as their advisor, they will be reluctant to make any decision that might conceivably hurt another. Ultimately, Amy and Alec might be more interested in pleasing others than in fully managing their assets.

Studies suggest that many advisors and salespeople are Amiables at heart. So, if you're interested in making friends, Amiables may be your best bet. But if you're interested in turning prospects into clients, it's best to cool it with the Amiables.

Top Answers

The second best answer to a "Yes" is a fast "No." When you get one, thank the prospect, and move on.

The key to dealing with Amiables is to be professional. Consider the good doctor persona again. While many doctors are cordial and pleasant, virtually all of them know when to flip that imaginary switch and get on with the business at hand. Doctors are completely serious about the importance of their work, and you should be unfailingly serious about yours, too, especially when dealing with the Amiables.

Since it is easy to waste your time with Amiables, here are a few questions to keep the relationship moving:

- Are we ready to proceed?
- Is there anything you need to know before we take the next steps?
- Is something keeping you from starting a relationship now?
- Is there anything you need to do before we can start working together? Can I help with that?
- Is there a problem in telling your existing advisor that you're making a change? Is there anything I can do to make that easier for you?
- Are there others in your family or professional advisory team you would like me to meet with to make you more comfortable with proceeding?

If, after you ask these kinds of questions, a prospect isn't willing to move forward but is willing to schedule a follow-up meeting, make sure he or she knows that the purpose of that meeting is to make a decision. Better yet, make that the purpose of a follow-up telephone call. Remember, sometimes the best next step is to stop pushing and lean back. Let prospective clients know you like them and would like to help their family, and that you will be there for them when they are ready to work with you.

THE ANALYTIC

He drives up in a Toyota Prius and walks into your office looking a bit disheveled. He wears a plastic pocket protector on his shirt. His Trios is on his hip, and an antique slide rule protrudes from his back pocket. OK, that's a bit over the top. Some Analytics wear Armani suits and drive BMWs. Regardless of how they dress or what they drive, however, Analytics are a special breed that need to be identified quickly and dealt with accordingly.

When Mr. Cocky brags, he brags about how great he is. Amiables are proud of their friendships and affiliations. Hobbyists show off their "gardens." When a Controller (discussed below) pounds his chest, he wants you to know how much better he is than you. Analytics rarely brag, but if they did, it would be about the processes by which they solved problems or found solutions.

In a world that many people see as gray, the Analytics tend to see in black-and-white. That difference doesn't particularly bother them, however, because Analytics, for the most part, are not people-oriented. They much prefer crunching numbers and reading the fine print to chatting about relationships.

When it comes to investing, they want tangible proof. Third-party endorsements help, but facts, figures, and flawless logic are better. The more statistics you have to corroborate your conclusions, the more likely the Analytic is to respond. Analytics savor solutions and abhor mistakes and errors in judgment. That's one reason why they may take quite a while to make a final decision.

Misconceptions about Analytics abound, however. They may not look the analytical type at all, and they aren't all engineers, either. While it is probably true that engineers are more likely to be Analytics, many engineers are not. And plenty of Analytics aren't scientists of any kind.

Also, while Analytics may bury their emotions more deeply than others, don't for an instant think they're bloodless, fully rational beings. In fact, one of your jobs as their advisor will be to get them to understand that investing is not always a rational process. While one likes to think that the investment markets are fully rational in the long run, few would argue that reason always prevails in the short run. Investors who don't understand the sometimes erratic nature of the present can get themselves into serious trouble.

It's an Emotional Decision

From the moment he entered the showroom, he made it clear that his purchase would be an entirely rational one. He was an engineer whose specialty was sophisticated medical devices. "I'm a completely rational buyer. This purchase will be based on the specifications of the car, the specifics of the financing, the comparative analysis of the various evaluation services— it's gotta be red— and the customer satisfaction ratings of your service department."

It's gotta be red!?! If that's not emotional, what is?

So much for completely rational decision making!

Scott, an advisor in Silicon Valley, is an expert in working with Analytics. "I have an advantage in working with the high-tech types. By training at least, I am one, so I know how they think, and I know the mistake most of them are making. They really believe that by breaking down an investment portfolio into its component parts and carefully examining each element, they can come to a definitive answer all by themselves. That's why they often fail to see the value of an advisor's contribution and hate commissions and fees.

"The first thing I do with them is satisfy their hunger for facts, figures, and tangible proof. At the same time, I'm also letting them know that I know what I'm doing, that I can be as analytic and process-oriented as they are. So I send them links to all kinds of Web sites and studies. We look at charts together and run sensitivity analyses. I create custom flowcharts to illustrate how different kinds of trusts will affect their estate plan or how different approaches to philanthropy will affect the charities they care about and their own balance sheet. At this stage, I ignore much of what I have learned about keeping things as simple as possible and speaking in plain English. Instead, I talk about alphas, betas, Sharpe ratios, residual correlations, and all that.

"Then I step back, shift gears, and try to put things in perspective. They have to understand that investing will never give them the kind of certainty they get solving a math problem. There are too many variables. So I ask them right out: 'What do you think the purpose of investment analysis actually is?' They usually try to come up with a textbook answer. Then I say, 'That's all good stuff, but that really isn't the purpose. Analysis is critical, but its purpose is not to find the answer. It is to narrow down the area in which you guess. Now, it is critical to guess in as small an area as reasonably possible, but in the end, anyone who thinks they are being entirely rational is kidding themselves. Another way of saying all that is that the final decision about any investment is not made in the head, it is made below the neck. It is intuitive.'

"Then I tell them the story of Seymour Cray and the gremlins. They all know Cray. He is a computer legend. He led the design team that created the world's first transistor-based computer and went on to be called the Thomas Edison of supercomputing. When asked what he did to generate new ideas when he reached a dead end, he teased one interviewer with this response, 'The gremlins tell me.' He went on to describe his hobby of digging underground tunnels whenever the ideas stopped flowing. He would dig and dig until the gremlins told him what to do next. In other words, as brilliant an analyst as he was, he still relied on an intuitive process."

So did Albert Einstein. "There is no logical way to the discovery of these elemental laws. There is only the way of intuition," Einstein said. When it comes to investing and life, there are too many variables for analysis to provide definitive answers. It's your job as an advisor to help the Analytic realize that.

Questions for Analytics touch on several categories. Some are designed to make sure you've satisfied an Analytic's need to understand what you're proposing. Others are in the hopes of getting past their linear process to provide a sense of their underlying emotions. Much like Amiables, Analytics often have a difficult time making a decision, and, left alone, can analyze forever.

A few questions to consider include:

- Do you see the logic of what we've outlined here today?
- Does the process make sense to you?
- Do you have a clear sense of what our working relationship would be like?
- Are you comfortable with the process and the plan?
- Are you satisfied that it can work for you over time?
- Do you see the need for any adjustments to meet your specific needs?
- Do you see how what we've outlined is better than what you're currently doing?
- Do you understand that the platform is flexible? If we start the process today, we can refine the plan and make adjustments in the future.
- I don't see any reason why we shouldn't proceed. Do you?

THE CONTROLLER

"If anyone is going to make a mistake managing my money, it's going to be me!" That's the Controller. Most clients will want some control over their financial future. That's healthy. After all, it's their money and their future. Controllers, however, are maniacal about it. Some will insist on doing everything themselves or micromanaging every step. A typical rationale: "That way, if I lose money, I won't have anyone to blame but myself."

Others may be willing to become your client but they will check, test, and verify everything you suggest. Their line: "I want the final say on everything that happens with my money, and I want to be involved every step of the way." They may not say that to your face, but their subtext will be something like, "How can I trust you with my money? Even in the unlikely event you are as competent as I am, you will not be as committed to perfection as I am."

Because they often come off as arrogant and demeaning, Controllers share some attributes with Mr. Cocky and the Cynic. As with other personality types, there are some important differences, though. Controllers are passionate perfectionists with a heightened sense of order. In addition, they have an intense need to direct the agenda–any agenda and every agenda. Interestingly, their swagger and roar and their need for control is usually driven by the desire to protect themselves from some deep-seated insecurity or fear.

Convincing a Controller to become a client can be a mixed blessing. Controllers rarely make great relationships because they can be nearly impossible to satisfy and frequently abandon an agreed-on strategy.

Stan, an advisor in St. Louis, relates this story: "I really thought I had won this client over. She was a handful, to be sure, but we agreed on a plan, and she even let me have discretion over part of her money. It was all working fine until one month when there was a computer glitch, and her statements got screwed up. Of course, I had nothing to do with it, but she went ballistic. Despite the fact that my firm straightened it out quickly, she pulled her account, saying, 'I knew I couldn't trust you to get it right.'"

Tim, a successful advisor in Los Angeles, easily recognizes the Controller because a number of his clients fit the description. One of those clients is the founder of a high-tech company; two others are successful trial lawyers; and another is a prominent Hollywood director. Why does Tim have them as clients when he doesn't need their business, no matter how significant? Controllers can be a handful, Tim agrees, but adds that he's learned to work with them.

"The first time I encountered one of these guys, he really got under my skin. He was a master at putting me down, and I took it personally. So I did a little research on control freaks and even talked with a buddy who's a shrink. Now, when they push my buttons, I don't let them get to me. I stay calm, centered, and on track. When they get haughty, I remind myself that I am not the target. They were like this long before I met them.

"My shrink buddy suggested I think of them as insecure and be patient with them. He also suggested I let them set the agenda at first, but that I set the pace by speaking slowly. I don't have a clue as to why that works, but it does. I start by assuring them that I understand their desire to control their finances. It is important. Then I tell them, that's why, when it comes to my clients' finances, I am a perfectionist. It is my profession and I take it very seriously. Then I shift gears and ask them a question. 'How would you feel about someone who asked their doctor how to lose weight and quickly added, "Don't tell me to eat less and exercise."' They usually chuckle. So I explain the catch-22: If they want to control their financial future, they need a full-time professional on their team. But to get a top-flight professional to work with them, they have to let go of control. I let that sink in a little and then add, 'The way to gain control is to let go of some control.' If we get past that point, I assure them that they will be in control of setting the direction and goals. My job would be to help set the plan and then carry it out. It doesn't always work, but it has gotten me a few big clients no one else could work with."

Columbus, Ohio–based advisor Phil, who earlier shared his thoughts on listening, offered this on dealing with control freaks, "When I meet prospects who want to be boss and insist on dotting every 'i' and crossing every 't' themselves, my first thought is that there is no way I can do a proper job for them, and it might be best to avoid them altogether. Then I give it one more shot. I call them out on it. I ask questions like:

- May I be brutally frank with you?
- Can I be completely honest with you?
- Can we be blunt with each other?

"Then I tell them that trying to control everything about their investments is going to eat their guts up and cost them a lot of money. To point out the absurdity of their position, I ask a lot of little questions. Do you:

- Grow your own food?
- Raise your own meat?
- Sew your own clothing?
- Build your own house?
- Mow your own lawn?
- Prepare your own taxes?

"I try to make it fun so they don't get the idea that I am in any way mocking them, because I am not. Their feelings are understandable. This is important stuff. My intent is to start a constructive and frank discussion to determine if I can help them."

Follow up your initial approach with more directness. For example, "I'm getting the sense that you like to be in control of everything all the time. That can be a serious stumbling block for me or any professional advisor because the markets are always changing and churning out surprises. We can work to manage risk, but nothing in the financial world can be completely controlled. If we work together, I will be your dedicated advisor, your personal CFO, but not a gofer. You will have to let me do my job, and sometimes I will make difficult recommendations that I will expect you to accept. If we can't agree to this set of ground rules, then I think it would be best for us not to embark on a relationship at all."

A risky approach? Perhaps. It certainly might cost you the account. But accepting anything less from the Controller probably won't work for either of you in the long run.

MS. PENNYWISE

"One percent? You're kidding! That's way too expensive."

That fee objection is almost always made by the ultimate Ms. Pennywise, who doesn't like to pay for anything. If that's the case, call her on it and deal with it, or forget it and find another prospect.

In most businesses, a percentage of customers have real price objections. They really can't afford that \$80,000 car, or the \$2 million house. When it comes to high-level financial advice, however, affordability is rarely the issue. Someone with \$1 million to invest can afford a \$10,000 fee. So why would they raise the question?

Often it's a ruse to deflect attention from the real issue: You haven't convinced the person of the real value of your services. Instead of scrambling or fishing when Ms. Pennywise balks at your fees, take the positive tack: "Actually, I'm proud of the fees we charge because they reflect the value of the service you will receive. May I explain why?"

Another advisor deals with fee objections by using an approach to a classic sales technique, the "right-angle close." This is when an objection gets turned around by posing it as a question: If the objection were not an issue, would you buy now? For example, "I understand you're concerned about the fee, but just so I understand your concern, if the fee were more to your liking, would you be ready for us to start working together on your affairs?"

If the person answers "No," then it's clear that the advisor hasn't convinced the prospect of the value of his or her services. If the answer is "Yes," then it may be that the prospect wants to avoid paying more than someone else for the same service. The prospect could also be testing you to see if your fees are negotiable.

In either case, try the proud-of-your-fees tack. "My fees not only are fair, they're an outstanding value for the service provided. Sure, you can get something somewhere else for less, but you get what you pay for!"

Pamela, the south Florida advisor with a practice specializing in retirees, has her own way of showing a prospect the value of her services while at the same time identifying whether that person is Ms. Pennywise. Pamela asks if the prospect has hired other professionals' services. For example, if the prospect just redecorated her multimillion-dollar home but refused to hire an interior designer, that decision tells Pamela something. If the prospect's elderly husband still mows the lawn, that says something, too. Sure, she might love decorating or he might see the lawn-mowing as exercise, but there's also a good chance these people hate paying fees. "When I get someone like that, I sell the value of an interior design firm and a lawn-mowing service first," Pamela says.

Interior designers, for example, typically charge a fee plus a markup on the furniture. But a good designer usually provides better results with less hassle or wear and tear on their customers' part and often saves them money in the end. More important, designers reduce the risk of a problem later and are there to help if one does surface. A quality lawn service doesn't come cheap, either, but it usually gets a better result and gives the customer more leisure time. If a person puts a reasonable price tag on the value of his or her time, hiring professionals usually saves money.

The Big Lie Versus the Big Truth

When advisors run into clients who don't like their fees, consider the following:

The Big Lie:

You can get the exact same service free or for half the price.

The Real Truth:

Your value proposition.

Among the questions to consider asking Ms. Pennywise are:

- Can you do all the investing and related money-management functions yourself?
- Do you have the same high-quality expertise as a team of professionals?
- How many hours a month will you spend doing it yourself?
- How much is your time worth on a per-hour basis?
- What's the total cost if you do it yourself?
- Do you think a team of professionals can achieve a better return than you? How much better?
- Do you think that as a professional advisor I would be able to either increase your return or protect you from making a mistake that would cost you more than the amount of my fee?

Perhaps you can get Ms. Pennywise to look at it another way. "I sometimes make the distinction between do-it-yourselfers and professionals by comparing investing in corrective eye surgery," says Pamela. "I ask them, 'Would you rather get Lasik eye surgery from the cut-rate corner shop or from a top-notch ophthalmologist?'" It's all about avoiding mistakes and ensuring peace of mind. "The majority of people who opt for the cheaper Lasik procedure do just fine. Only a small incremental percentage will have a problem. But the more expensive surgery nonetheless is worth the price because you don't want a problem in the first place, and second, if a problem should develop, you want the very best doctor to deal with it," she adds.

In that sense, hiring an investment advisor is like buying risk-management insurance, with the advisor's fee as the premium. In a bull market, the do-it-yourselfer or cut-rate advisor may yield acceptable results, but what happens when things go wrong or get tough? Value isn't defined by the easy stuff–it proves its worth in the difficult times. Let's face it. Most of what a medical doctor does day to day can be done just as well by a nurse or a physician's assistant. So why bother with the doctor or question his or her fees? Because we want the best we can get, just in case. That's also

why we carry insurance on our cars, homes, healt
not have the same mindset with investments?

BEYOND THE PERSONALITY

Now that you know more about how to identify and understand investment personalities, the challenge is to look beyond superficial facades. You will want to see and understand your clients' investment wiring—the baggage they carry around that relates to money and the underlying drivers of their unique behavior toward money. Again, asking the right questions can help, including:

- When it comes to money and your finances, what worries and concerns you? Why?
- What are your earliest recollections of money?
- Can you tell me about your parents and money, and their wealth or lack of it, their spending habits?
- How did your parents feel about money? Was your parents' business life or career stable or volatile? Did they move around a lot? Are they still alive? Has their attitude toward money changed over the years? Did either of them gamble?
- When you were a child, did you get an allowance?
- What chores, if any, did you do to get that allowance?
- Did you have a job when you were in high school or college? What did you do? Do you remember what you were paid?
- If you have children, how do you handle money with them? Do you give them an allowance? Do they work for their allowance? Have they ever had a job? Would you in any way want them to?
- Do you speak openly about money with your children or in their presence?
- Are your children enthralled with all the gambling on the Internet or with the poker craze? Do you think they participate in any way? How do you feel about that?

- Do you and your spouse or partner ever argue about money? If so, what do you tend to disagree about? Does it happen often? How do you resolve your differences?
- In what ways do you and your spouse or partner feel differently about money?
- Have you, or anyone in your family, ever had a significant financial reversal? A bankruptcy, loss of job, significant reduction in income or net worth? At what stage of life did it occur?
- What prompted the setback? Whose fault was it, and how did it affect you?
- In dollars, how much money would you like to have?
- Are you rich? Do you feel rich? How much money will make you feel rich?
- What do you consider the major accomplishments of your life?
- Have you ever had any major disappointments in your life as a child, in high school, and later in life?
- Is there anything else in your life experience, your relationships, your hopes, dreams, or fears that might affect your thoughts about money and investing?

YOUR ROLE: ELIMINATE EMOTION FROM INVESTING

Getting past your clients' façades and exploring their investment wiring is not an end in itself. Our only objective is to help you help your clients get the emotion out of their investment decisions. Financial advice is not psychotherapy, however. Our interest is in identifying and controlling the underlying emotional drivers that compel less than rational investment behavior.

"Controlling client emotions is the most important, as well as the most difficult, part of the job," says Andy, an advisor in Indianapolis. "I've found that when a prospect tells me they've lost a big chunk of their capital, they're concerned about more than money. Their ego is at stake. They start thinking about other times they've lost something in their lives and get even more upset. I had one prospect who admitted that he had insisted his last advisor take very aggressive positions, but when he lost, he went into a tailspin. He told me it reminded him of having lost the big game when he was a high school basketball player. I felt he was blaming his former advisor for that, too. What has a basketball game played 35 years ago got to do with investing today? That doesn't make sense, even here in Indiana, where basketball is king."

The answer to Andy's question should be "Nothing at all." Yet investment wiring is unpredictable, and in this case it seems to have mattered quite a bit.

People can be emotional and irrational in good times as well as bad. "When things don't go our way, some clients make no secret of the fact that they think it was my fault," says Andy. "But when it's good, well, it's as if they get a whiff of their own perfume and fall in love. All of a sudden they have the Midas touch, so, just when the market is about to turn, they want to place bigger and bigger bets. When it is up, they take all the credit. When it goes down, it's my fault. That was always a complete mystery to me until a few years ago when a client told me his parents always praised him for everything and never made him accept responsibility for things that went wrong."

One area in which emotional baggage likely will have significant impact on a client's financial future is when dealing with concentrated wealth. This kind of wealth can be created in a number of ways, from the vacation home that's increased in value to the point that it dwarfs the client's other assets to a single stock position inherited from grandpa to a windfall received in exchange for the sale of a small business or created from years of service with a successful company.

"When most people in Silicon Valley think of the way people fall in love with a single untouchable asset, they focus on young tech millionaires," says Bob, an advisor in San Jose, California. "While it can be difficult to persuade them to diversify, the toughest cases I have come across have been UPSers who received a windfall when the company went public. Those folks are attached. 'I drove that truck for 30 years. UPS has made me wealthier than I ever could have dreamed possible. I love UPS and will not sell a dime of that stock.' You can shout Enron and WorldCom until you are blue in the face, and they won't hear you."

There are ways to get clients to think differently about their beloved stock or untouchable asset, however. McCauley and McGuirk did it when they got their client to start talking about *a* stock, not *my* stock.

David Ferris, a wealth advisor with Merrill Lynch, provides advice to a small and select group of wealthy families with several hundred million dollars in assets. He is accustomed to dealing with the challenge of concentrated stock. His approach involves offering a "gift" to the client who insists on concentrating his or her wealth, but the gift is contingent on one thing: they must agree to invest the entire gift in a single stock. For example, if they have perhaps $25 million in a concentrated stock, Ferris offers to write them a check for $25 million on the condition that the entire $25 million is invested in one stock of their choosing. Then he asks if the stock they selected is their company. "So far it never has been," Ferris adds. "That question has a way of cutting through all the emotional attachment issues that often keep a client from making the obviously rational decision to diversify," he says.

As you begin to move beyond your clients' investment personalities to their particular investment wiring, you are in uncharted territory. While it is legitimate to wonder if clients who share a general personality type will have similar investment wiring, the answer is not predictable. As we've mentioned several times, while certain patterns may exist, the specific possibilities are endless. As an advisor, you must evaluate each client individually. Enjoy the adventure.

RISK TOLERANCE

Perhaps the most significant impact a client's wiring has on his or her investing is its effect on risk tolerance, the amount of risk the client is willing to accept when it comes to his or her money. As one advisor describes it, risk tolerance is what clients are willing to do and still be able to sleep at night.

An individual's risk tolerance can change substantially at different times, in various markets, and in differing situations. The reasons for those fluctuations change, too. People often overestimate their tolerance for risk while they're making money in a bull market and become too conservative in a bear. They also tend to be more conservative as they get older, especially when they retire. Ralph, an advisor in Vancouver, British Columbia, Canada, offers another reason for variations in tolerance levels: "I meet with a client over lunch and together we calmly assess his or her risk tolerance. We sort it all out and then go to work on a rational plan that takes into account what my firm calls the client's 'investment personality.' We agree and get started . . . . Six months later, the client hears a few guys in the locker room at the gym saying the world is coming to an end or tech stocks are hot or whatever, and all bets are off. As a result of that overheard conversation, the client decides to change his or her risk tolerance."

Barbara, the Phoenix advisor mentioned in the past chapter, points out that personal tragedy can change a client's risk tolerance, too. She recounts the tale of a 30-something client of eight years who had had good success with an aggressive investment approach. Then his dad died suddenly. "Overnight my client became very conservative. We talked about it, and it wasn't that he had less money. In fact, there was a fairly large inheritance coming his way. If anything, he now had the money to take even greater risk. It was that his father had been his 'rock.' It had been easy for him to take risks in the past because he knew his father would be there to pick up the pieces. Now Dad was gone."

This client's investment decisions were driven by his investment wiring, not his needs and goals or any rational assessment of the market. We'll talk more about the intricacies of risk tolerance in Chapter 5.

THE TAKEAWAY

- When dealing with understanding your clients' investment wiring, good enough isn't good enough at all. It's not enough to know a client pretty well, be comfortable with him or her, and have the client be comfortable with you.
- The job of a great advisor is to probe deeper and deeper until he or she understands how a client thinks and feels about money and why.
- Most of the time in everyday life we deal with personality façades. That works at social gatherings and even in our daily lives. But when it comes to serving your clients or building a meaningful advisory practice, don't settle for superficial relationships.
- Getting past a client's façade and into his or her investment wiring should lead to having a client for life.

Chapter

4

WHAT'S THE PURPOSE OF MONEY?

Money is a personal matter, and so is whatever you or anyone else wants to do with it. Great advisors know that. They also know the questions to ask to help steer their clients to the right financial decisions for their situations with their ultimate purposes or visions in mind.

Advisor Lori Van Dusen opens conversations with new clients with the question, "What do you want to do in your life?" Top financial advisor Frank Patzke, of FP Financial Services, always asks his clients, "What worries you?"

How an individual answers these questions usually opens the door to fruitful exploration of their feelings about money and its purpose in their lives.

Wise Words

I finally know what distinguishes humans from the other beasts: financial worries.

Jules Renard, *19th century French writer*

It sounds so simple, yet it's not. The classic approach many advisors take with new clients is: "Tell me about your goals and objectives." Standard questionnaires also ask clients to list and then prioritize "goals and objectives." Yet too few advisors bother to ask their clients directly what they want to do with their money. Or if they do ask, they fail to follow up the answers with more questions that dig deeper.

Wayne, an advisor in Salt Lake City, explains that often when he asks clients, "What's your money for?" they look at him blankly and then reply, "Everybody knows what money is for." Then, without taking the time to reflect on it more deeply, they say something about buying material goods, sending the children to college, or retiring someday.

But Wayne doesn't let his clients dismiss the question that easily. "I explain that there's nothing more important for us to talk about than how they view the purpose of money. It is a critical and necessary steppingstone to building a financial plan and sticking with it.

"If you ask a working man or woman living from paycheck to paycheck about the purpose of money, they have no trouble telling you it is for food, rent, the shirt on their back, and maybe an occasional trip to the doctor," says Wayne.

Ask someone with old money, and they usually have an answer that has been refined by the family over generations, he continues. "I worked with one family that had a mission statement that was passed down and refined over several generations. It discussed the family's priorities regarding their commitments to their church, the community, and a number of charities. It also set out broad investment guidelines on how the money was to be managed," he adds.

"When I ask people in the affluent middle class, the so-called mass affluent, about the purpose of their money, they talk about everything from taking cruises to buying cars, vacation homes, and college for their kids or grandkids. They tend to talk about things," Wayne continues. "The key is to get those people to talk to you and then get them to focus on the deeper issues."

To help a client, we as advisors have to know and understand exactly why that client is investing, he adds.

A DIFFICULT CONVERSATION

Don't expect these conversations with clients to be easy. They're not, and clients often resist the discussion. Typically, they're not deliberately hiding anything; they just probably never thought about the purpose of money in this context. Some clients may insist that this kind of conversation is meaningless and a waste of time, but most will be willing to talk. They may have a difficult time formulating answers, too. Be patient. Let them know that in order to help them, you must know them. Your role is to find creative ways to encourage them to explore more deeply. Perhaps that means repeating or restating a question, drawing on examples from your own life, or, without revealing any confidences, sharing the experiences of others.

These advisor/client discussions are important because they get to the heart of why an individual wants to invest. As an advisor, this is precisely when you must practice that art of listening. As we've talked about, open your ears and listen for clues to what really matters to each client and why. In these discussions pay careful attention to what a client says, how he or she says it, and what's left unsaid. Actively engage your client in a serious, deep, and high-level conversation with a full and open exchange of ideas, opinions, and feelings about money.

Ask the right questions, listen to your client's answers, don't jump to conclusions, and then gently probe further. Remember, getting a client to open up starts with your own attitude. Make sure you stimulate the conversation, not stifle it.

As you discuss the purpose of money with a client, you'll probably have to direct the conversation a bit more than usual. That's in part because the distinction between goals and purpose can be a bit elusive for many. If a client repeats his or her goal and has trouble digging deeper toward the purpose, take a leadership role but don't actively lead your client. Instead, facilitate the discussion with open-ended questions such as:

- Can you tell me what's behind that goal?
- What does that goal mean to you?
- How would you feel if you achieved that goal?
- How would you feel if you didn't?

"Most people haven't really thought through the purpose of money in their lives," says Carolyn, an advisor in Westchester County, New York. "They are too busy making, spending, and worrying about it. I see a big part of my contribution to my clients as getting them to slow down a bit and be a little introspective. Before we can plan, they have to decide what they want money to do for them. Once they've established that, together we can set priorities. There is no point in working 24/7 and investing every dime, just to head off in a direction you don't want to go or, worse, to arrive someplace you didn't want to be."

PURPOSE VERSUS GOAL

When you first ask clients to be specific about the purpose of money for them, they usually come back with comments such as:

- Buy a dream car, boat, or RV
- Pay for the children's college
- Have a $5 million net worth at retirement
- Travel the world

But these specifics are not purposes. They're merely goals or ways to spend money once it's acquired. Each goal is tangible, with a clearly defined endpoint. Such goals also are what many people give as the reason for investing.

A purpose, on the other hand, goes much deeper. It's not an end. It's a direction you would like to take over the long haul with specific goals serving as mileposts along the way to help monitor your progress. Purpose sets the context within which priorities are determined. For example, if you're in New York, and your purpose is to head west, Chicago could be a goal. Once in Chicago, you still can go farther west. Similarly, if a client's purpose is to become wealthy, having $5 million could be a goal. And once that goal is attained, you can set higher goals.

It's vital to have both goals and a purpose or vision, and it's just as important that you and your client address them in the proper order. Understanding why you want to have money comes first. Once that's clear, it becomes the context in which to create a meaningful financial plan with set goals and priorities. Putting purpose first makes decision making much easier.

For example, if a client says she wants $3 million in her retirement plan by age 62, that's a goal. If she says she wants to be free of money worries by retirement age, that's a purpose. To have well-educated children is a major purpose of money. A related goal within that context could be to save the money necessary to send your children to college.

When Lisa, an advisor from Cincinnati, asked her client to paint a vision for her future, she responded with a detailed description of an imaginary vineyard in the Napa Valley. The new client, Mary, was a 49-year-old, midlevel corporate executive who had been recently widowed. "Mary had an incredibly clear vision of this vineyard down to the kinds of grapes she would grow and the view from her house on the property," says Lisa. "As she described the place, I had a passing thought about wanting to visit it. I knew that the vineyard was a goal and not a purpose, but I didn't want to say that yet. To begin with, I didn't want to rain on her parade. She had such a good time describing it. More important, I needed to learn more first."

So, she asked Mary a series of questions:

- How did you come to have such a vivid vision?
- How long have you been thinking about this?

- Is this something you and your husband talked about before he passed away?
- How do you think your life would change if you could snap your fingers and be in the vineyard today?

Mary's answers to those questions helped Lisa understand what Mary really wanted in her life. She didn't want to be a world-class vintner or to make the best wines in the world. She wanted a change that would allow her to get off the corporate ladder and slow down.

"So, Mary," Lisa went on, "can you see that the vineyard is really a goal–a lovely goal–but a goal? Reading between the lines, it appears you just told me that one purpose of your money right now is to give you a way to slow down. As I listen to the passion you have for this vision and your answers to my questions, I think you are saying that you would like to slow down sooner rather than later. Is that right?"

Mary's response, Lisa says, was, "How about today?" Given Mary's financial situation, Lisa knew that her job then was to help her client consider alternative goals that she could realize more quickly and that would still accomplish her underlying purpose.

Rick, an advisor in San Diego, adds his take on goals versus purpose: "I'm retired military, and one of the first things they rammed into us at the Academy was the difference between your overall mission and the strategy and tactics you might use to achieve it. When planning a battle, or an investment portfolio, first you have to define your mission. Then you decide on the specifics of how you will get there. When it comes to investing, you have to know your purpose, the general direction in which you are headed. Next you assess your resources, and only then do you determine your route."

Consider those "lucky" people who win lottery jackpots. Perhaps they're not so lucky after all. Many of them, like most people, seldom have a clue to the real purpose of money in their lives. As a result, they often end up back where they started–the money is gone and they're left with little or no nest egg. That happens because they satisfied goals without a purpose.

Advisor on the Hot Seat

What's the purpose of your money? As advisors, ask yourselves that question first.

Says Andy, an advisor in Indianapolis: "I was like the doctor who doesn't take care of himself, the lawyer who dies without a will, or the accountant who files his own taxes late. I was so busy trying to get clients clear on the purpose of their money that I never bothered to get clear on the purpose of my own. One day, a client turned the tables on me, and asked, 'What's the purpose of your money, and do you and your wife agree?' I did a good job scrambling for an answer, and she seemed satisfied. Fortunately, I didn't fool myself. So my partner and I took each other and our spouses through the process. It not only helped me personally, but it also made me better at helping others."

A few questions advisors can ask to help clients recognize the real purpose of their money include:

- What are you hoping your money will accomplish for you?
- Why do you need money to do that?
- What benefits do you expect from money?

Be careful, though, not to ask clients only about their goals, cautions Eric, a Los Angeles–based advisor and a rising star with the securities arm of a major bank. "Discussing goals limits the conversation," says Eric. "Asking about the purpose of their money is much more open-ended. It gets them to open their hearts and allows me to become more intimate with them right off the bat."

Ross Mayer of Commonwealth Financial Group recounts asking one couple what their money was for. The husband replied, "Isn't that obvious? We want to be able to retire." When Mayer pointed out that retirement was more of a goal than a purpose, the man's wife tentatively said, "We want financial security when we both stop working." After getting the husband to concur, Ross then asked how much money the couple thought they'd need to feel secure. The clients couldn't answer that, so Mayer moved on. "Perhaps that is why you are here. So we can sort it all out together."

Mayer didn't push the issue further at the time because he truly was *listening* to his clients. Mayer says he sensed that the husband was getting impatient, and so, knowing there would be plenty of opportunity to revisit the issue later, he moved on.

Emotional eloquence not only is about asking the right questions and listening to the answers. It's also about knowing when to back off. "I knew this couple was going to be a project. The husband is a real 'cut-to-the-chase' bottom-line kind of a guy. His wife is the exact opposite. She's ready for conversation. My hope is she will work on him and make the process easier," adds Mayer. "In any event, you can't expect to get everything done in the first meeting."

BEYOND SIMPLE ANSWERS

Don't automatically accept a client's initially stated purpose of money, either. To provide the right financial guidance, you may need to learn much more about the client and his or her real purposes. One way to help determine if you're getting the whole scoop from clients and prospects is to look at what they are currently doing with their money. Sometimes that can paint a better picture than what they say they want. One of the most common examples is that of the couple who say they want financial security and education for their children, but keep spending money on vacations and adult toys.

"There's an old saying that goes, 'Show me what you have, and I will tell you what you really want,'" says Debra, an advisor in southern Connecticut. "I doubt that saying holds true in all aspects of life, but it certainly plays out with the way many people manage their money. For example, they'll tell you that their money is for security, and then they go out and buy a new Porsche. I have built my career by getting people to say what their money is for, and then comparing it with what they are actually doing. I take what they say and contrast it with their budget, spending habits, and current assets. I see myself as holding a mirror up to their faces that forces them to see what they are doing."

Debra recounts the story of a couple who didn't want to part with their second home, a beachfront property on Cape Cod. It wasn't that the couple viewed the property as a getaway spot, as some advisors might assume. Rather, they saw the property as a way to gather the family together. Here's their discussion on the purpose of money and the home's role in it all:

Debra: What is the purpose of money for you?

Husband: I want to retire at age 62 with $4 million in investable assets over and above my personal real estate.

Debra: That is really a goal and we can work on that, but first, I want to understand what the purpose of money is for you.

Husband: Well, I guess it's to be financially secure when I retire.

Debra: OK. But let's go further. What does security in retirement mean to you?

Wife: We want to maintain our lifestyle, not worry about health care, and be able to leave something nice for the children and someday–hopefully–grandchildren.

Debra: Sounds good. Now please tell me more about how you visualize your life in retirement.

Husband: We will probably sell our house and replace it with a similar home in a warm climate. Of course, we'll keep our waterfront house on the Cape for the summers.

Debra: Well, I can certainly understand your desire to get away from these winters. I'll be right behind you someday. But let's talk about the house on the Cape. As I remember it, you said it was worth a little over $3 million . . . That house is the bulk of your net worth right now. Isn't it?

Husband: Yes, but I see where you're going, and we're not going there with you.

Debra: Look, I can't touch that house or anything else of yours. It's yours, and all decisions about it will be yours. I'm just here to talk it through with you and make sure you do what you and your family want long term.

Wife: The house on the Cape is more than a house. It is a fountain of family memories and a source of joy for all of us. It's the family jewel, and we are not touching it.

Debra: OK, but please, so I can understand your situation, just tell me one more thing: Looking into the future to your retirement, just what is so important about that house?

Husband: My wife and I see it as the gathering place to which my children and, eventually, grandchildren will return every summer. That house will keep our family together long after other families have drifted apart.

Debra: OK. Now I understand why it is so important. Before we go on and start talking about some specific goals and priorities, let me summarize the answer to the question about the purpose of your money: To provide security for both of you in retirement and to allow you to maintain and nurture your relationships with your children and grandchildren to come. Does that work for you?

Debra's client couple, like many people, have what Bob, the previously mentioned advisor in San Jose, California, refers to as a sacred cow in their portfolio. "It could be a vacation house, stock holdings concentrated in a family company, or even an inherited portfolio that Grandpa said never to sell. Whatever it is, understanding the client's real motivation for the holding, the true purpose for the client's money, allows for a meaningful conversation about the client's real priorities," adds Bob.

In the case of Debra's client, they haven't sold the Cape Cod house yet, but Debra did persuade them to cancel a major renovation and invest the money instead.

When talking with your clients about the purpose of their money, often they will give you the answer they think you want to hear—which is not necessarily the truth. "It's for the children," they'll say, or "We want it for our retirement," then they'll jet off to Europe first-class, stay at the Ritz, and forget funding their pension for the year. Clearly, they weren't honest about their vision for their money, and it becomes your job as their advisor to find out what that purpose really is.

If a client's consuming, saving, and investing profiles are consistent with what he or she tells you is the purpose of his or her money, then you're ready to move on in the planning process. If not, you need to press more deeply.

Remember advisor John Rafal and his tack of asking clients about their parents and siblings? Rafal says he counts on the answers to such questions to provide essential insights into a client's background, and, in turn, to help him identify inconsistencies in their money persona. That's the approach he used with Karen, his client we discussed earlier.

San Jose advisor Bob recounts another case of contrasts. He had a 46-year-old client who talked the game, but behaved very differently from his stated purposes. The client said he wanted money for financial security in retirement, but his spending patterns suggested something else. "When I asked if his parents were still alive, the mystery was solved. Both of his parents had died before their 40th birthday, and his older brother, a marathon runner, 'bought the farm' at age 49. While he was reluctant to say so, the client obviously was convinced that he didn't have too long to live. I took a risk and pressed further by asking how his parents and his sibling had died. His father had been a heavy smoker and died of emphysema and lung cancer. My client didn't smoke. His mother died of a heart condition that could have been controlled with modern drugs and surgical techniques. And his brother had been hit by a car while running at night. While his conviction that he was going to die early made emotional sense, logic suggested he would be around a lot longer than he thought."

Self-Worth and Money

For better or worse, money goes a long way to defining who we are and where we stand in our community. This makes for an explosive combination that can lead to very expensive consequences, both financially and emotionally.

UNDERSTANDING PRIORITIES

Advisors shouldn't assume their clients have a clear sense of priorities for their money. Remember the newly retired doctor and his wife with about $2 million in their portfolio and grandiose ideas on what they could afford in their retirement? The doctor faced the prospect of going back to work if the couple didn't trim their expectations and prioritize what really was important to them.

The vast majority of high-value prospects and clients today are aging baby boomers—among those 76 million people born after World War II and through 1964. Those boomers, as we all know, come with "consumption" as their middle names. "I want it all and I want it now" was, and still is, their mantra. Many have pocketed substantial earnings over the years. Yet they tend to have more memories and material goods than bulging investment portfolios. Also, for many, investing today has become a game of quick catch-up to build retirement nest eggs without giving up anything. As their advisor, it's your job to contrast what these boomers say is the purpose of their money with the current realities of their financial picture. Purpose can provide the context for a discussion of priorities.

Consider this experience with a new referral. Art, the advisor in Baltimore we mentioned in Chapter 2, told us this story: "The prospects wanted our second meeting to be at their home because they needed to be available for any questions from the various contractors working on a substantial renovation. When I arrived, a late-model luxury SUV in the driveway was parked beside a brand-new BMW 750Li. . . . Contractors were putting the finishing touches on granite work in their newly remodeled kitchen and baths," says Art.

"We immediately jumped into a discussion of the purpose of money to them. Every word out of their mouths was about security, peace of mind for the future, taking care of the children, and so on. They were both midlevel executives in their early 40s who wanted to retire by age 62. Their investment portfolios were as paltry as their home and cars were grand. I decided to show them that I was deadly serious about the importance of what I do for clients. So I went right to the core. 'That's a beautiful new 750Li in the driveway,' I said. The client proudly stated that he just had received an $80,000 bonus and decided to treat himself. I pulled out my calculator and did some quick math, then said: 'In round numbers, had we instead invested that money for your retirement, that $80,000 might have grown to $500,000 or $600,000 by the day you retire.' There was a long uncomfortable pause. After a while, I decided to let him off the hook a little by saying, 'Look, it's a great car and you should enjoy it. But if I am going to be your advisor, when you get a chunk of cash in the future, or even if you get the desire to buy a new toy, I want you to call me so we can discuss it in light of the way you define the purpose of money for the family. Right now, let's talk about what other purposes you might have for your money.'"

To provide a better sense of understanding the difference between purposes and goals, we asked Rick, the retired military officer mentioned previously, to share a client scenario and conclusions. First, Rick says, he starts his planning process by examining the client's purpose, goals, and priorities. Then he turns his client's attention to the subject of risk. (We will focus on risk in the next chapter.)

Following are excerpts from Rick's notes and conclusions about one couple. (It's all disguised, of course, to preserve client privacy.)

Facts

- Seemingly happy married couple
- Ages: husband, 52; wife, 51
- Projected remaining life expectancy: 40 years based on second to die
- Children: Four, ages 22, 19, 16, and 9 (jokingly called "Oops")
- Income: husband, $350,000, with 7 percent projected annual increase; wife, none
- Status of employment: stable
- Projected retirement age: 65
- Primary assets:
  - $1 million liquid
  - $3 million equity in family retreat in the Rocky Mountains, in the family for two generations
  - $500,000 equity in primary residence
- Estate and insurance planning: Adequate and continuing to fund
- Future inheritances: None of consequence expected
- Future obligations (known): Ten more years of college. Four years will be paid for from a separate college fund; the unfunded portion amounts to $250,000 in current dollars.
- Focus: Couple agrees they have enough toys and want to start to focus on financial security for the future.

Purposes and Goals

1. Purpose: To fulfill their sense of duty toward their children and meet their parental obligations to educate their children
   - Goal: Fully pay for the best four-year institution that will admit each of their children
   - Goal: Help pay half the cost of any graduate education for their children

- Goal: Help with down payment on first home for each child

2. Purpose: To maintain core family traditions
    - Goal: Keep the house in the Rockies
    - Goal: Pass the house in the Rockies down to future generations
    - Goal: Enjoy annual family vacations
3. Purpose: To have a secure retirement
    - Goal: Pay off the mortgage on their primary home
    - Goal: Have 70 percent of their last year's working income available for retirement per annum
    - Goal: Have flexibility to retire at age 62 if desired

Though fact patterns vary, these clients face a very typical dilemma, says Rick. After going through the process of defining their purposes and the associated goals, the need to set priorities becomes clear. "For my next meeting with these clients I prepared a number of scenarios based on their current situation and varying investment return assumptions, and their short-term, mid-term, and long-term needs as indicated by their time horizon."

As with many clients, the couple will need to prioritize because it's likely they won't be able to meet all their goals, Rick adds. "We almost certainly will have to revisit their purposes and see if there is another way to fulfill at least some of them."

Ego and self-worth issues can be powerful forces that may conflict with other purposes of money. Don't assume your clients have a clear sense of what they really want to do with their money.

San Jose advisor Bob takes an approach that helps his clients stay with their stated purpose: "Once my clients and I have identified the purposes, set the goals, established their priorities, and agreed on a plan, I insist that they run all their major purchases by me before they act on them. I'm not the enforcer here. I just remind them of what they said they wanted and help them pencil out the impact of these decisions. As an advisor, you've got to be careful that you're not seen as a killjoy or, worse, as an arbiter in their marriage."

Says Heather Walsh, "My partners, Stephen DiCarlo and Jody Chadwick, and I find that while there are clear exceptions, when we discuss purposes and goals with married couples, it's usually true that the husband will be very clear on his goals but vague on what we even mean by purpose. The wives tend to be the opposite."

For example, she recalls meeting with a couple where this difference became a serious problem. For more than an hour the couple debated their purposes and goals, yet the gap between the husband's and the wife's ideas seemed to keep growing exponentially. Knowing that her job was to pique the couple's interest in this type of conversation to help them sort out their differences, Walsh gave the couple a homework assignment: come up with a joint vision of their retirement years. Her intention, she says, was to use the vision to help the couple start setting their priorities. The need to get the couple to agree on a vision for their retirement was essential, given the realities of the couple's resources and their desire to upgrade their lifestyle.

The couple came back a week later even further apart on their visions, says Walsh. "Steve, Jody, and I talked about it and decided that this was a disaster waiting to happen. We smiled a little as we realized that earlier in our careers we would have taken them on as a challenge. Now we know better, so we decided to pass. We didn't want to be marriage counselors."

Advisor or Therapist?

Do you ever feel like a surrogate therapist or even a marriage counselor to your clients? How deeply you probe your client's psyche is up to you. But keep in mind that unless you're trained as a therapist and hired as such, it's best to focus on those issues related to a client's purpose for money.

FAMILY MATTERS MAKE A DIFFERENCE

So, some prospects can't agree on their purpose. Another client resents that her brothers had inherited the family business. All the siblings but one want to sell the family's vacation home on the water, but the one won't sign the papers.

Family members can disagree on everything from whether to sell the family business to politics, religion, and what charities to support. As an advisor, never overlook the importance of family interactions and their impact not only on investment wiring but on a person's perceived purpose of money.

Remember Walt from Chapter 3? He's the advisor from Maine who talked about dealing with the different ideas about money among couples and multiple generations in families. Sometimes their money baggage fits the stereotypes of husbands and wives, and sometimes it doesn't, says Walt. The husband may be cheap and the wife a spendthrift, but it could easily be the other way around. She may be risk averse while he likes to gamble, but that's often not the case as well.

Lori Van Dusen sees a big part of her job as an advisor as building consensus. "Consensus building is as important to do with a family as it is with the board of trustees of a major institution," says Van Dusen.

The question is, How do you build that kind of agreement? Ralph, an advisor in Vancouver, British Columbia, Canada, says he starts by explaining to the husband and wife that he works for both of them, not just one of them. The two have to find enough common ground for him to do his job, Ralph adds. "I had this one couple who couldn't agree on much of anything. A particular point of contention was a condominium they owned in San Francisco that had soared in value. He wanted to sell it; she wouldn't hear of it. They got so upset discussing it in my office, I was about to give up on them. Coincidentally, two days earlier I was at a meeting where a woman gave a speech on settling political issues. She talked about how mediators use common-ground techniques to reduce differences on issues as touchy as abortion and gun control. They get opponents to see that they at least have some common views. For example, in the case of the abortion debate, by definition neither side wants unwanted children. Similarly, both the defenders of the right to bear arms and those who advocate gun control can agree they do not want guns in the hands of criminals.

"I figured if common ground was a place to start in hypersensitive issues like those, maybe there was hope for this couple," adds Ralph. "So I gave it one more try. I asked them to tell me what the condo meant to each of them. Given how upset they had been, I thought it had something to do with the fact that she had dual citizenship and wanted a stake in the United States. But that wasn't it at all. They both saw it as an investment, so one step at a time we worked backward to find their point of difference. It was like peeling the layers off an onion, so it took some time. It turned out that their only difference was that she thought the San Francisco market would keep on growing, and he thought it had topped out and was incredibly risky. Once we discovered that difference, we worked on a couple of others. The process got easier, and I asked them to finish resolving their differences at home. It worked."

Solving family differences is rarely easy, but it is crucial. Great advisors remember that.

THE ROLE OF TIME

What is a client's time horizon? That's perhaps the most typical question in client questionnaires, and it's among the least understood. Even advisors don't all agree on what it means. A time horizon can be everything or anything from how much longer clients will be earning money to how long they have to allow their money to work and grow to how long they'll need their money based on life expectancy projections to their types of goals–short term, midterm, or long term.

Let's consider what a client's time horizon may mean in light of a series of questions that great advisors ask their clients in order to gain perspective on an individual's situation:

- How much longer do you wish to work?
- When do you want to retire?
- Do you want to work during retirement? If so, full-time or part-time?
- What's the typical longevity in your family? This can help us get a sense of how many years we will need your money to work for you.
- How old are your parents, or how old were they when they died?
- How is/was your parents' health?
- How is your health?

For many people, the purpose of money is security and peace of mind over some specific time period. Often, they are too short term oriented in their view. They tend to focus more on now and less on later. Depending on a client's financial situation, you as an advisor may or may not be able to provide them the "now." But you can help them build for the future by helping them set their priorities and start on a plan.

The head of sales for one of the country's most successful managed-money marketing organizations teaches his sales staff this approach: "Say your father died of natural causes at 84, and your mom died of natural causes at 88. You are 63 and in good health. Most actuaries would tell us to average your parents' age at death and then add four years. In your case, it would be very reasonable for us to project that you will live at least until 90. So if you want to retire in two years at 65, that's 25 years in retirement that we should plan for, at a minimum. Now let's add your spouse's life expectancy into the equation."

All this leads to the intersection of the purpose of a client's money and the client's short-term, midterm, and longer-term goals. For example, clients may say the purpose of their money is security and peace of mind so they can afford to retire with a comfortable lifestyle. They also may have a short-term goal of taking a global cruise next year and a midterm goal of five years down the road upgrading their second home to a beachfront property. If you have a clear sense of your client's overriding purpose for their money, you're in a better position to help them approach their goals realistically and stay on track with their purpose.

WHO IS YOUR REAL CLIENT?

As you sort through a client's financial goals along the path to achieving his or her purpose of money, conflicting needs often arise. That's when it's essential to know your real client. No, we haven't lost our marbles with this one. Not only do you want to help your clients clearly understand their priorities, you also want to lay the groundwork that will allow you to speak up when they get off the track from their stated financial purposes and goals.

Of course, in a real sense your clients are the people sitting in front of you. But there's almost always more to the story than that. Your client also may be that same person across the desk in 10, 15, or 20 years. The client of today may well have different wants and needs from the same client years from now. Your client also could be the children or grandchildren of that person across the desk, or perhaps even their aging parents in need of care.

As Bob, the advisor from San Jose, puts it, "I ask them who they want my client to be. Then I go on to explain that I must know who it is I am supposed to protect (financially). Is it them now, them later on, their children's education, or someone or something else?"

Take the example of a client, Nancy Jones, 50, divorced, with a grown daughter and a $1.5 million nest egg. She has a secure job, earns in the low six figures, and enjoys a good lifestyle. If you think about it, she really doesn't need an advisor right now. But Nancy, at 50, with money in the bank and a good source of current income, isn't the ultimate client. Instead, the real client is the

Nancy a number of years down the road in retirement who will need to rely on her investments to supplement her pension to continue the lifestyle she's accustomed to enjoying. Your ultimate client also might be Nancy's daughter or grandchild, for whom Nancy might want to ensure financial security thanks to a sufficient inheritance.

Just to make things more difficult, you, as an advisor, often may find that Nancy at age 50 with her spending habits may be the enemy of Nancy at age 75. Your job as her advisor, then, is to take care of the elder Nancy even if it means confronting and challenging the younger Nancy when necessary.

Says Dale, an advisor in Orlando, "As an advisor I see the essence of my role as protecting my clients' long-term financial future by being the advocate of their primary purpose as they have defined it. That often means that I temper their desire to spend lavishly today or allocate their investments too conservatively or aggressively. So I ask them, 'Will you empower me as the guardian of your long-term financial future?'"

THE TAKEAWAY

- Great advisors aren't satisfied with merely helping their clients set a series of goals. They know that goals are temporary, easy to set, and easy to change or drop.
- Purpose endures and is much more lasting than a goal. An individual's purpose is analogous to an institution's mission or even a government's constitution. Of course it can change, but amending it is a serious undertaking.
- Purpose establishes the context within which the financial planning process takes on its meaning. It focuses the plan, the advisor, and the client on what is truly important. And then it keeps everything moving in the right direction–the same direction that the client set after deep reflection.

Chapter

5

WHAT ROLE DOES RISK PLAY?

Helping your clients understand and deal with risk is a critical aspect of providing financial advice. The concept of risk permeates client relationships from prospecting to planning, execution, and ongoing client service and reviews.

But what exactly is risk and how can you help your clients comprehend its significance? As we'll discuss throughout this chapter, risk comes in all shapes and sizes, and means different things to different people in different situations. People measure risk in several ways, too. Often risk has negative connotations, especially those relating to the loss of money. However, risk can encompass market volatility and the loss of opportunity, as well. In other words, risk isn't necessarily bad. In fact, in many cases, it's an essential part of helping clients achieve their financial goals.

"Every client contact relates to a discussion of risk," says advisor Paul McCauley. Let's look more closely at why risk plays such a dominant role.

TODAY'S DYNAMIC

Helping your clients understand the role of risk is especially important with today's rising demographic tsunami and the pressures on the nation's traditional retirement support system. That three-legged support system includes a Social Security system under stress, company pensions that in many cases no longer may be guaranteed, and personal savings–which, today, often are nonexistent or vastly inadequate.

The tsunami lurks in the wave of 76 million baby boomers–those people born from 1946 to 1964–who are turning 60 at the rate of nearly 8,000 people a day, and are either retiring or nearing retirement age. Many have unrealistic expectations of how they will fund the rest of their lives, grandiose dreams of what they plan to do, and only meager savings. In case that's not a challenging enough picture, medical breakthroughs mean that boomers will live longer than their predecessors, thus requiring financial support for years beyond those of previous generations. In some instances, people today will end up being retired longer than they were in the workforce.

Beyond these mass affluent boomers (we define them as people with $100,000 to $3 million to invest), older people also need help steering their financial courses. They have their own set of obstacles and risks, beginning with soaring medical costs and lost or jeopardized pensions. Their sound financial futures may be in jeopardy, too. All this and more contributes to the challenge that you as financial advisor face when guiding your clients to deal with risk and, in turn, make the financial decisions that are right for them.

ESSENTIAL RISK

We all know that some degree of risk is a necessary part of successful investing. Too much risk, however, can feed the flames of a reckless portfolio that then crashes and burns. Risk is the oxygen of an investment portfolio, says Dave, a top advisor in Nashville. "It's an essential element for a portfolio to breathe and grow. The problem is that fires need oxygen, too. A big part of my role is to find precisely the right mixture so my clients' portfolios breathe but don't burn."

"Unfortunately, left to their own devices, investors rarely get the risk mix right," adds McCauley, in accord with his partner, Gary McGuirk. "In a bull market, clients almost always overstate their ability to withstand risk. In a bear market, they're much less willing to accept risk because the memories of being bitten are too fresh," says McCauley. "So we ask them right out, 'Does your appetite for risk change based on the environment?'"

Great advisors not only manage the risk in a client's portfolio but also recognize their client's tolerance for uncertainty and loss as it relates to money, and then successfully use that risk to their client's financial advantage.

John, the Atlanta advisor, describes what he calls his clients' *mailbox risk.* Many people are afraid to open their mail and read their statements, he says. In fact, some never do. "I ask them, 'How can I help you so you will never be afraid to open your mail and read your statements?'"

As an advisor you can help your clients understand that with your help and guidance, opening the monthly statement doesn't have to be a painful jolt.

Joan, an advisor in lower Manhattan, talks about a client couple who failed to learn a tough lesson on risk, were whipsawed, and paid twice over. "In our last meeting my soon-to-be clients had opened their financial hearts to me. They told me about the financial and emotional roller coaster they had been riding: how they pounded their chest with confidence and glee while they calculated their gains as the bull market roared; the losses and pain they suffered when the bear market crushed them; and how they quickly realized that they were really not the aggressive investors they thought they were. As new converts to conservatism, they dove on what cash they had left, only to miss the recovery due to their newly discovered risk adversion. They were both 52 years old, and their big concern now was retirement."

In the next meeting with her clients, Joan pointed out that the first step was for them to learn from their experience and gain some perspective on risk so that the mistakes of the past weren't repeated. She then helped them face the harsh reality of what their risk aversion cost them. "Bluntly, your current financial picture, the way you have painted your vision of retirement, and your notions about risk are at odds. We have to sort all that out before we move forward."

The Sleep Quotient

It's taken me 37 years of this business and of watching people get beaten up to understand one simple truth: If you cannot sleep with your portfolio, you will never enjoy your return. There are no perfect answers, but what's critical to learn is your [client's] sleep quotient.

—Ross Mayer, Commonwealth Financial Group

As Joan knows, discussing retirement and the often necessary investment risks with affluent boomers makes for tough yet worthwhile conversations. As with Joan and her clients—as well as with many others—after you, the advisor, analyze the situation, you must show your clients the clear need that they either accept more risk of volatility and potential loss, or accept the fact that they must alter their vision of retirement.

The good news is that more boomers are open to getting help from a professional and have a more flexible view of retirement than do preceding generations. Numerous studies indicate that many boomers plan to continue working in some capacity beyond age 65.

George Burns on Aging

- *Retirement at 65 is ridiculous.*
- *When I was 65 I still had pimples.*
- *I can't get old; I'm working . . .*
- I can't die, I'm booked.
- *I look to the future because that's where I am going to spend the rest of my life.*

—George Burns, *comedian who died at age 100*

PERCEPTIONS OF RISK

Individual perceptions of risk vary dramatically and can change like lightning, as Joan's clients discovered. Those perceptions aren't always as expected either, so great advisors must pay attention and listen closely to their clients. Brian, an advisor in Colorado Springs, Colorado, recently ran into one of those unexpected perceptions when he asked prospects at a seminar what risk meant. "I had a fellow in his 80s enthusiastically throw up his hand, and then blurt out, 'Opportunity.' He later told me that he saw risk as exciting."

Not all seniors have such an optimistic perception, however, and it's often challenging to talk about risk with older clients. They've been around long enough to have experienced plenty of boom and bust, and usually are weaned on two beliefs about investing:

- Buy and hold
- Think "fixed income" in retirement

Of course, as advisors we recognize that both tenets carry big risks. "Buy and hold" has allowed many investors to accumulate substantial holdings in a small number of stocks, but it also comes with inherent risks that include lack of diversification, risk of emotional attachment, and risk of inertia because of imbedded, unrealized gains and therefore significant tax costs if and when the stocks are sold. Many older investors are reluctant to sell their concentrated stock because they know that after they die, their heirs will benefit from a stepped-up basis. While this is a valuable tax advantage, these days, with the original owner likely to live much longer, the risk of waiting for a step-up is much greater.

The move to fixed income, too, has left many seniors vulnerable to a low interest rate environment. It puts them at risk of outliving their money, being forced to scale back, or, worse yet, having to ask their children for financial help.

Among your responsibilities to your clients is to show them—no matter their age, financial standing, or outlook—a picture of their financial futures under different sets of assumptions about inflation rates, savings rates, withdrawal rates, investment performance, asset allocation, and more. Often the numbers will produce an answer your clients don't want to hear. But it's reality, and you must help them confront it, understand it, and plan accordingly.

"Many of my clients remind me of when I was obese," says Wayne, the Salt Lake City advisor. "I'd go to the doctor and say, 'I have to lose weight, but don't tell me to exercise and eat less.' Many clients want to have a comfortable retirement at an early age, leave a nice legacy for the kids and grandkids, and spend all their income maintaining their current lifestyle. Something has to give."

Remember the recently retired doctor with the $2 million portfolio we met several chapters back? No matter how much he and his wife didn't want to hear it, their financial reality meant scaling back or returning to work, and his advisor wasn't afraid to tell him so.

Many of today's boomers face that same harsh reality. Because they've failed to save adequately or haven't managed risk properly, they're faced with the options of working longer before retiring, working during retirement, cutting back their lifestyle now, cutting back later, or managing investments and risk more wisely.

TOLERANCE FOR RISK

Great advisors realize the importance of correctly recognizing the level of risk that's acceptable to a particular client. Without that, it's virtually impossible to design a financial plan that truly will satisfy the client and meet his or her needs. Making your job more difficult, your client may not recognize his or her true risk tolerance because often it's profoundly influenced by that often elusive investment wiring we talked about in Chapter 3. It's up to you to understand that, counsel them, and offer the appropriate guidance. It will help the client and thus cement a healthy, long-term relationship with them.

A few of the typical questions that many advisors ask in the hopes of digging deeper into their clients' risk psyches include:

- What does risk tolerance mean to you?
- What is your risk tolerance?
- Can you rate your risk tolerance on a scale of one to ten?
- Looking at four alternative investment-return streams over five years, which would you prefer? Each has a different degree of volatility and annualized returns.

"These kinds of boilerplate questions that most of us ask are helpful," agrees Sheila, an advisor in Portland, Oregon. "But they don't go nearly far enough. Determining a client's individual notion of risk is one of the most important things I do for my clients. When pressed, I've found that most clients don't really know what 'risk' means, don't know what 'tolerance' means, and certainly don't know what the combination means. I wasn't even sure I did. So I looked it up in a securities textbook:

> *Risk tolerance is an investor's willingness to suffer one or more declines in the value of his or her investments while waiting for them to increase in value. Risk tolerance can be measured in either absolute or relative terms.*

"That clarified it a bit for me, but wouldn't really resonate with the majority of my clients," adds Sheila.

So instead of walking clients through dictionary definitions and most likely not getting very far, try equating risk and risk tolerance to clients' lives with the help of more questions.

- To what degree are you willing to deal with a drop in your portfolio? What about repeated drops?
- Have you ever lost any serious money? In other words, enough money that it affected your lifestyle, plans, or sleep?
- If not, do you think that investment losses would affect your overall spirits, sleep habits, relationships, health, or work? To what degree?
- Has anyone in your family or close to you lost any serious money? If so, how did that loss feel to you? Did it affect your actions with regard to money?
- Are you willing to take on more risk for something you truly need as opposed to something you merely want? How about the other way around? Are you willing to assume more risk with discretionary income usually spent on non-essentials or toys?
- Do you and your spouse or partner see risk the same or differently?
- Do you care more about how well you do in terms of dollars accrued or how well compared with your friends and family?
- Which is more important to you, beating the market or meeting your goals?
- Do you regard financial risk solely as the loss of money? Or do you consider lost opportunity a form of risk, too?

Later in this chapter we'll take a closer look at how people view risk and lost money versus lost opportunity. But first, let's look at yet another risk-related obstacle advisors must add to the financial planning equation.

CHANGING TOLERANCES

Perhaps one of the biggest deterrents to a client achieving long-term investment success–and possibly your retention as their advisor–is the variability in their risk tolerance. We talked a little about it in Chapter 3, but, simply put, clients change their minds on how much risk they're willing to accept when it comes to their investments. Not only do they often mischaracterize their tolerance for risk up front, but that tolerance vacillates as markets fluctuate, the clients age, and as their circumstances change. In Chapter 3, Ralph, the Vancouver advisor, ran into a client who flip-flopped on risk tolerance after overhearing a conversation at his gym. A client of Barbara's, the Phoenix advisor, changed from aggressive to conservative with the death of his father even though his portfolio was unaffected.

Glenn, an advisor in Tucson, Arizona, explains yet another way that clients' risk tolerance changes. "Often you find the sheep in wolves' clothing. In order to get the upside, clients say they are aggressive investors who can handle market downturns. Then, the moment the market heads south, they call you up, claim they are conservative, and want to abandon the plan. So," he continues, "when the market starts wreaking havoc on their portfolios, I need to be there to remind them of the purpose of their money as they defined it and the danger of abandoning their plan. I need to protect them from their natural instinct to want to hunker down and protect."

Then Glenn recounted an all-too-typical story about his client Ellen. When she first started investing, taking chances was a snap. The markets charged ahead, and she felt she had little to lose and a world of time to make up for any losses. Ellen began to equate risk with fast and easy reward. For a time, her risk-taking approach worked and she enjoyed heady profits. In fact, the more Ellen earned on her investments, the more she wanted. Then the markets tanked, and Ellen discovered the dark side of risk. Her investment account lost more than 90 percent from its high point and cost her half her original investment.

When Ellen finally came to Glenn for help, she was humbled and scared. The problem was that she had become too conservative and, try as he may, Glenn couldn't get her to position herself for the next upturn. As a result, she missed the opportunity to recover at least some of her losses.

RISK OF LOST OPPORTUNITY

Lost opportunity apparently doesn't seem to bother investors in the same way that losing actual cash does. Studies show that the majority of investors feel much worse about losing money they once had than they do about losing money they could have had if they had acted differently. Nonetheless, advisors shouldn't overlook those successful high achievers out there who are at least as concerned about the risk of lost opportunity as about the risk of losing what they already have.

David Ferris addresses this issue head-on. When meeting with a client whose net worth is vastly overweighted in a concentrated stock position that is currently trading at, say, $10 a share, he asks, "Which would make you feel worse? If you don't sell any of the stock and the price goes down to $5, or if you do sell and it goes up to $15?"

David says that he finds that this question goes to the essence of a person's underlying attitude as it relates to risk. "While many people only view a tangible dollar loss as a setback, a lot of the people I deal with have even more of a problem handling missed opportunity. If I do what we all know is the right thing and get them to diversify by selling some or all of their holdings at $10 and it goes to $15, the 'woulda, coulda, shoulda' eats them up at night. They obsess about how much money they could have made if they just hadn't listened to me. Others will sell the stock and be happy with the gain and never look back."

Those clients or prospects who focus on opportunity often are reluctant to diversify a concentrated holding. Sometimes they simply fail to see the risk. That's true whether their holdings are concentrated in a single stock, in a business they've built, or in real estate holdings that have treated them well thus far. As their advisor, you can help them by asking questions such as:

- What's the point of all this concentration?
- To what end are you taking all this risk?
- What if the stock craters?
- What if the competitive landscape shifts dramatically for your business?
- What if the real estate cycle turns again?

Someone else who may have trouble diversifying a concentrated holding is the client who still doesn't understand the purpose of money. Bob, the advisor in San Jose, recounts meeting with a Silicon Valley prospect who started their conversation with the question, "How much are you going to tell me to sell?" The prospect was a senior executive of a high-tech company whose stock, it turned out, was at its peak. Everyone kept telling him to sell at least some of his $25 million in vested holdings in the company, especially because he had plenty of options yet to vest and very few other assets. "Nobody could get him to sell a share," says Bob. "In this case, it wasn't just that he could only see opportunity. It was that I couldn't get him to articulate any purpose for his money. He was a bachelor techie living in a rented apartment, and he just didn't seem to care. He rode the stock down to zero."

ABSOLUTE VERSUS RELATIVE RETURNS

Further complicating your job as an advisor is the fact that clients' risk tolerance can be measured in either absolute or relative terms. Is the client more concerned about how he or she is doing in terms of dollars and cents–that's absolute return–or how it relates to various market indexes–relative return?

Eric, the Los Angeles–based advisor we mentioned in Chapter 4, used to ask his clients to peg their risk tolerance on a scale of 1 to 10. But then he says he realized that all the score provided was a sense of those clients' perception of their risk tolerance. "It told me next to nothing about their actual risk tolerance. I still ask for their score, but I follow up by asking this: 'If we embark on a relationship today, how much money can we lose before you fire me?' Then I contrast that answer to their 1 to 10 score. The 6, 7, or 8 they gave me usually has to be adjusted downward to a 3, 4, or 5."

The client who says his risk tolerance is high but then turns around and says he'd fire an advisor who loses 10 percent of his money reveals much about his real risk psyche. Obviously, the client should have scored his risk tolerance much lower. Less apparent, however, is the likelihood that the client is more concerned with absolute results rather than relative ones.

To help determine your clients' attitude toward absolute and relative issues, you might follow Eric's lead and ask your clients how they would respond to relative setbacks. For example:

- You say you would fire me if you lost 10 percent, but what if the market was down 20 percent? Would you still dismiss me?
- What if the market was up 10 percent and we were up only 5 percent? How would you feel then?

Obviously, if a client tells you that you're fired after a 10 percent loss and then reverses that if you add the additional information that the market was down 20 percent, relative returns carry some significance. If the additional information doesn't change the reaction, then absolute returns are most likely paramount.

Typically, the investing public has been conditioned to focus on returns relative to various measures of the market. What did the Dow do today? How about the NASDAQ? These are the normal questions many people ask. The problem with that perspective is that relative returns don't buy houses, don't fund your clients' children's education, and won't pay for their retirement. Absolute returns do.

Of course, when evaluating the performance of a money manager, relative returns are relevant. Oversimplified, if markets are down 20 percent and an equity investor is down only 12 percent, that investor probably did something right. Maybe his or her money managers did a good job or maybe the investor's mix of different types of equities cushioned the downside. Reality, however, is that the investor is still down 12 percent. He or she just lost $12 on every $100 invested. That's absolute return–or lack thereof.

As one investor put it, "When someone tells me I should be happy because I lost less than the market, it reminds me of what the grocery cashier says when I buy groceries: 'Because you're a member of our shoppers' club, you just saved $4.93.' No I didn't. I just spent $64."

PERSONAL MEASURES OF RISK

While both relative and absolute returns have their places in terms of clients achieving their goals, absolute returns are paramount. That's because once you've helped your clients determine the purpose of their money, set their goals, and lay out a plan, the most important issue becomes whether the client achieves the absolute return targeted by the plan. Nonetheless, always ask your clients: if your plan requires an *x* percent return per year for you to achieve your goals, would that be your only measure of success? If not, how else would you measure success?

If their response is that they would compare it to one or more market indexes or to how their friends' and family's investments performed, you will know that relative returns are important to them.

Rarely do clients see the targeted absolute return as the most important measure of success. Instead, here's a simplified version of what happens. Assume that the investment plan you put together for a client calls for minimizing risk, a diversified portfolio, and a targeted return of 7 percent per year. The portfolio achieves 8 percent. Congratulations should be in order. You've done your job well, surpassing your goal. Instead, a well-publicized investment style like small-cap growth records a 25 percent rise during the same time period, and suddenly the client wants to abandon other styles and chase that winner.

Misguided Mantra

Many investors, left to their own devices, won't stay with their plans. These are the same people who don't invest when the ship is moored at the dock, and instead wait until it pulls out to sea to jump in the water and swim after it. Then they wonder why they get soaked.

Compounding the problems you as an advisor must deal with to do the right job, many clients will change their positions on relative versus absolute returns. When the market heads up, they tend to demand their fair share relative to what everyone else is doing. When it's headed down, they absolutely do not want to lose money.

Specifically, advisors often talk to their clients about *upside/downside capture ratios*. In plain English that refers to what the portfolio likely will do if a market goes up or down. For this purpose, the market may be defined as a particular stock index or a composite benchmark that reflects the mix of indexes mirroring the client's proposed strategy. For example, if the upside capture ratio is 100 percent, the client expects that his or her results will mirror any gain in the market. If the downside capture ratio is 80 percent, then the client supposedly is insulated from 20 percent of the downside move.

In actual fact, that would be quite an accomplishment–the investor gets all of the upside but, because of the way the account was managed and diversified, is exposed to a lower percentage of the downside. Many investors will be satisfied on the upside, but may not be fully prepared for the downside. After all, while they're insulated from 20 percent of the downside, they can still suffer 80 percent of the decline. Should that happen, the bottom line is that they will lose money–less money perhaps, but it's still an absolute loss of money.

Commonwealth Financial Group's Ross Mayer puts it succinctly. "Ratios are statistics. Hard dollars are real."

"The biggest single problem I've seen clients run into is that they overfocus on the upside and accept too much risk initially," says Martin, an advisor in Seattle. "When the going gets tough, they make the second and perhaps bigger mistake of bailing from their plan at precisely the wrong moment. To make sure my clients understand what all the ratios mean, I take a page from the hedge fund people and put it in tangible absolute terms. They use terms such as *drawdowns, recovery periods,* and *high-water marks.* In [plain] English, I look at how much money a client would have lost in the worst stretch of time and how long it would have taken for them to recover the losses, and ask the client if they could live with that. If the client can't, I adjust the plan before the fact, rather than after," adds Martin.

Often when investors should be most fearful, greed rules instead, and when they should grab up the bargains, they run for the exits. Think the technology boom and bust of the late 1990s.

Larry, an advisor in Warwick, Rhode Island, scribbles a squiggly line on a piece of paper, then points to it and tells his clients and prospects that it's the most important thing he's seen in his nearly 40 years in the investment field. That's not a typo either, so feel free to be confused–just as Larry's clients are, until he adds, "Things go up and things go down. And then they go up again and then they go down again. When they are going up, the biggest experts in the world tell us they will continue to go up–roughly–approximately–forever! And when they are going down, the same people will tell us that they will go down until they are dead. But that is rarely what happens. Things go up and they go down and they go up again. The key for us is to buy low and sell high," adds Larry. Then he goes on to explain that most people make the mistake of misinterpreting that to mean buy at the lowest point and sell at the highest. That would be great, but nobody can do that, says Larry. "We just try to buy low and sell high. That's what diversification and rebalancing are all about."

Powerful Ideas II

Those who do not read and understand history are doomed to repeat it.

—Harry S Truman, *U.S. president, 1945–1953*

Considering that in the past advisors often used fear and greed as a way of generating commissions, it's striking that one of the distinguishing characteristics of great advisors today is that they work hard to eliminate fear and greed from their clients' investment decisions.

Frank Patzke recognizes that fear and greed motivate much client behavior and also cause many problems for ill-advised investors. Part of Patzke's job, he says, "is to try to allay a client's fears and minimize their greed."

That's a Herculean task when markets soar, and greed often dominates investors' emotions, distorts their judgment, and clouds their vision. Left to their own devices, investors mistake the likelihood of loss as an exciting opportunity for great gain, a sure thing. They equate foolish risk taking with cunning, courage, and conquest. When the market is near a peak, telling a client that a hot stock is in fact risky actually may make them more eager to invest. That certainly was the case in 1999 with the dot-com IPO craze. It was also the case when certain hot condo markets showed signs of peaking in early 2005.

Illness forced Harry to retire just as his earning capacity peaked. While he had a decent nest egg, it wasn't nearly so much as he had thought he would have. But his advisor created a diversified investment portfolio that would keep his income adequate for his needs and provide modest growth for the future. Everything went well until the tech rally heated up. At first Harry accepted his advisor's advice to stay with the plan. Eventually, however, Harry was overwhelmed by jealousy and greed. Saying that he had to have a piece of this tech market, he fired his long-term advisor and gave all his money to a hotshot manager. A year later, he had lost more than half his money.

Harry's advisor had tried to talk him out of moving his money, but to no avail. The advisor kept saying "It's a bubble" for so long that he lost his credibility with his client. Worse, the advisor lost his credibility with himself, and he made the tragic error of starting to move some of his other clients' assets into tech. Fortunately for the advisor, however, the Internet bubble burst before too much of his clients' holdings had been moved into tech.

LONG-TERM GOALS AND RISK

Theoretically, we all know that investing is generally for the long haul and that, over time, markets go up. But the actions of very few people reflect that knowledge. "Almost everyone says they are a long-term investor, but few act that way," says Lisa, the advisor in Cincinnati we mentioned in Chapter 4.

When the market turns and major losses are realized, investors instead either freeze in the headlights or run for the exits, and almost always suffer a double whammy—the loss from a collapsed market and the loss from their newfound risk adversion.

At both the top and the bottom of the market, only a handful of investors have the presence of mind, the courage, and the right advisor to help them rebalance their portfolios in accordance with their long-term goals. Great advisors know that rebalancing is the most reliable way to ensure that their clients avoid the trap of buying high and selling low. Instead, it forces them to stay with the plan and, as we've talked about throughout this book, keep emotion out of investment decisions.

"Many prospects could be likened to vegetable gardeners who are so concerned about how the carrots are doing that they dig them up daily and examine the roots," says Lisa. "Then they wonder why they get wilted carrots . . . and wilted investments. So I

Wise Words II

A portfolio is like soap. The more you touch it the smaller it gets.

ask them, 'If you planted a garden and examined the roots every day, what would happen to your carrots?' It helps me make the point that both vegetables and investments need time to grow and flourish."

That's why advisors should take a page out of the institutional investment consultant's play book and draft individual investment policy statements for each of their clients. Make sure the client reads the policy statement, agrees to it, and then signs it.

It makes for fewer headaches in the long run, and actually can help a client stay with his or her investment plan.

Excerpt From Investment Policy Statement

We are risk averse and will not be able to tolerate an absolute loss in the portfolio that exceeds 15 percent of our original capital, no matter how temporary that loss may be. We recognize that this risk aversion limits how well we can do when the markets go up and are willing to sacrifice significant relative and absolute upside in return.

Signed and dated by Joe and Mary Client

CONSERVATIVE VERSUS AGGRESSIVE

As you have seen in the previous pages, becoming too conservative an investor after being burned in a bear market is usually a misguided approach. The potential risk can be as bad as or worse than the risk associated with making a bold move. For example, a client who is overly averse to taking investment risks could fall short of financial goals and dreams because he or she wasn't aggressive enough in investing.

Wayne, the advisor from Salt Lake City, shared a personal story that dramatically illustrates this. He was working with yet another couple burned by the tech bust of the past decade who were clinging to their remaining cash. Unfortunately, though, says Wayne, unless they invested at least half their portfolio in equities, everything they feared would happen to them in old age was likely to occur.

"At the time, I was about halfway through an exercise and diet regimen . . . so I shared my story," says Wayne. "When I first started trying to exercise, just going for a walk around the block took my breath away and made my heart beat like a Geiger counter in a radiation lab. I got scared and stopped walking. When I told the doctor about it, he said, 'You're right. There's a chance you'll have a heart attack walking around the block. But if you don't start walking around the block, you almost certainly will have a heart attack in the next few years.' I told my clients that just as my doctor was a professional and got me on the right track for my long-term physical health, I would have to do the same for them and their long-term financial health."

Ed, a seasoned advisor in Raleigh, North Carolina, told us of a client couple who insisted they were risk averse in the extreme. Their portfolio was about 90 percent fixed income. After their initial meeting with him, Ed knew that their view of risk would be a major obstacle to accomplishing their long-term financial goals. At the next meeting, to the couple's shock, Ed turned the definitions of conservative and aggressive upside down. "Based on what you have told me, I do not agree that you are conservative investors. I am sure that comes as a surprise. You both obviously consider yourselves conservative because you are taking so little risk with your current assets. That, however, is precisely the reason why I don't see you as conservative. As I'm sure you know, by definition conservative [investing] has to do with preservation. To date, your concern has been solely with preserving your assets as they are. I see the issue quite differently, however. My focus is to consider the likelihood that you will achieve your goals and be able to preserve your vision of your future. So the reason I do not consider you conservative is that, in my professional opinion, the probability of your succeeding is quite low. In that sense, at least, I do not see your decision to stay almost entirely in fixed income as conservative. I see it as aggressive. It may help you sleep well at night but that's only because you haven't played out the impact of your decision on your future."

Ed appreciates that conservative and aggressive are merely arbitrary labels with different meanings depending on one's point of view. The definition depends on individual circumstances. For this couple, taking into consideration the likelihood of achieving their goals, their investment tack was extraordinarily aggressive.

Perhaps the best definition of an aggressive investment stance, then, is one that has a low probability of achieving a person's financial purposes and goals and also preserving that client's vision for the future.

Classic questionnaires ask people to prioritize their goals among capital preservation, income, growth and income, growth, or aggressive growth. Unfortunately, with some advisors, if capital preservation is the top choice, the client can end up in a dead-end portfolio with little chance of loss *or* growth. On the other hand, great advisors recognize that while capital preservation is important, so is the preservation of the client's vision of his or her future.

Another approach that many clients think is very conservative but in reality is aggressive is when they focus their investments in the same company or industry that generates their income. Too often a residential Realtor's portfolio concentrates on rental houses, a pharmaceutical representative invests only in drug companies, and a software engineer buys only computer stocks. That can make for a volatile mix and undue risk.

If you run into clients who don't think this concentration is a problem, suggest that they talk to investment real estate professionals about what happened to them in the late 1980s and early 1990s when the bottom fell out of the investment real estate market, or to computer systems consultants after Y2K, or to the tens of thousands of tech mavens in the know who lost all or most of what they had in the dot.com bust.

Nonetheless, some people still will want to stay with an industry or company they know, or in a position with which they've grown comfortable, rather than adequately diversify. "Even though I have seen it literally hundreds of times," said Paul McCauley, "it still amazes me how clients who have a huge percentage of their money concentrated in a single stock they've owned for years think they're being conservative. They say, 'It's performed fantastically,' or 'I know the company and the industry inside and out,' and so on. Worse, many of them not only have virtually all their money tied up in that industry, but their expertise and their income, too. I guess at some level, I understand. But many of them see themselves as taking a conservative stance. They aren't. To help them see that, I ask a lot of 'what ifs.'"

- What if an Enron buys the company and milks it dry?
- What if technology makes its basic product obsolete?
- What if the bottom falls out of the industry, as happened to the airline industry after 9/11?
- What if your expertise is devalued and becomes worthless?
- What if your assets, your income, and your expertise all lose their value at the same time?

FAMILY MATTERS II

Finances are a family matter. Whether the issue is the purpose of money, the willingness to accept risk, buying or selling a security, or dividing an inheritance, consensus among family members is necessary to ensure a plan's success.

And, as we all know, building consensus isn't easy. "I hate to break it down by gender," says Lori Van Dusen, "but the difference I have noticed is that men seem much more likely to view the loss of opportunity as a major risk, whereas women seem more concerned with actual losses. While that seems to be changing with some couples, I am continually surprised by how common it is. I'm not sure why, but my theory is that men tend to be the ones who made most of the money, and they tend to think they could do it again. In fact, in cases where the women were the primary source of income, the issue seems to evaporate. Whatever the reason, getting the typical couple to a middle ground about risk can take some work."

Barbara, the Phoenix advisor, asks couples a raft of questions about their respective reactions to different eventualities. For example, "How would you feel if you lost 25 percent of your capital?"

"That helps," she adds, "but I find it more fruitful to ask questions that seem a little far afield":

- Do you ever go to Las Vegas or other gambling venues?
- Which casino games do each of you like?
- Who is the more enthusiastic gambler?
- Do you gamble differently when you're ahead than when you're behind?
- Do you set limits on how much you're willing to lose?
- Do you set limits on how much you'll win before you quit?
- Do you quit when you say you will?

"I'm never really sure what I'm looking for with some of those questions," says Barbara, "but the conversations often prove revealing. The answers to those questions tell me a lot about how they will deal with risk in their investment portfolios, and indicate the differences that need to be resolved."

THE PORTFOLIO ISSUE

Many investors also make the mistake of assessing their overall risk on an investment-by-investment basis. In other words, if they are extremely aggressive in the traditional sense, they want every position to be a highflier. If they are traditionally conservative, they want every single investment to be conservative. But risk and reward should be managed at the portfolio level. Great advisors make sure their clients understand that and also alert them that they will never be happy with every single individual position in their portfolio or with every slice of their investment pie.

"Every advisor I know talks about portfolio diversification as the antidote to risk," says advisor Wally from Walnut Creek, California. "After all, a diversified portfolio that is periodically reallocated and rebalanced is the way to enhance returns and still reduce risk. If you think about it, however, that means that, by definition, if clients are happy with every single aspect of their portfolio, they probably aren't adequately diversified. I tell my clients up front that if we do our job right together, they will be well diversified. If they are, there will always be something to be unhappy about in their portfolio. If I don't warn them up front, they will want to load up on the winners and dump or fire the losers. Often, that is precisely the wrong thing to do."

Risk management ultimately rests on wringing the emotion out of financial decision making. It's about creating a plan and staying with it. It's also about getting clients to recognize that their instincts and habitual views of what to do under various market conditions are often 180 degrees from what's in their best interest. Great financial advisors understand this and make it clear from the beginning that a critical part of their role is to manage risk. Often that means protecting the client from his or her own emotions and habits. In good times it's protecting them from their greed; in bad times it's from their fears; and all the time from any unrealistic expectations they may have.

IMPORTANCE OF EDUCATING CLIENTS

As you've seen from the various stories and advice throughout this book, educating your clients on all the varieties and variations of risk is essential to help them achieve their purposes and goals, and is crucial to their ultimate satisfaction with the job you

Thoughts On Value Propositions

What's your value proposition? Here are some good answers:

- I'm a risk manager.
- I protect my clients from blowing themselves up financially.
- I help clients wring the emotion out of financial decision making.
- I help clients maintain an even keel.
- I help clients keep their expectations in check.
- I get the fear and greed out of investing.
- I maintain the discipline to rebalance portfolios in good times and in bad times.

do as their advisor. For many, Risk 101 class starts with making certain they understand the difference between needs and wants.

Joan, the advisor in Manhattan, sees that distinction as a big part of her job. "I have to make sure they understand the difference between what they want and what they need. Many of my clients tell me they need things that they really only want. One not-so-silly example was a couple I was working with who could never seem to save any money outside of their pensions. I noticed they often talked about how great the restaurants in Manhattan are. I asked them how often they eat out. They said just about every night . . . [and] their average bill with wine and tip was somewhere between $125 and $150."

With a little quick arithmetic, Joan showed the couple that they were spending around $50,000 a year in restaurant bills alone. Of course, they need to eat, but by controlling their want to eat out at fine restaurants all the time, they easily could save and invest $25,000 or more every year.

The Ratchet Effect

- Knowing that a luxury once experienced becomes a necessity, many great advisors focus their clients on budgeting.

Confusing needs and wants is only one of the key misunderstandings people have relative to risk. A laundry list of other risks and concerns requires you as an advisor to educate your clients. Some of those include:

- A narrow view of the definition of risk.
- Worrying about remote risks while ignoring more urgent ones.
- Not truly understanding conservative versus aggressive investing, as discussed previously.
- Failing to recognize the impact of time on risk.
- Measuring risk inappropriately.
- Seeing risk as an individual investment issue rather than as a portfolio issue.
- Not understanding the impact of family matters on risk.

Don't overlook risks associated with financial planning or a lack thereof, either. A few of those concerns include:

- When is the last time you reviewed your will and trusts?
- Are your life and disability insurance adequate?
- Are you planning on receiving an inheritance? What is the risk it won't be what you think it will?
- Is it possible that your parents will live long enough that any possible inheritance is depleted?

Next come the omnipresent but rarely discussed risks associated with catastrophes, natural and otherwise. (These risks should be discussed even if your firm does not offer specific solutions for all of them. They are important and discussing them will show you care about your client's overall financial well-being.)

- How prepared are you for a major catastrophe?
- If a hurricane Katrina or some other natural disaster happened to you, would you be flexible enough financially to deal with it?

- Have you accounted in any way for the threat of terrorism in your financial plan?
- Could your plan survive a major economic setback?
- How would you feel if your beach house (remember those "sacred cow" holdings we talked about) were destroyed and along with it a huge chunk of your assets?
- What liability limits do you carry on your car insurance?
- How much umbrella insurance coverage do you carry?

Risks to a client's psyche can be among the most challenging and should be discussed:

- How would you and your family emotionally handle a significant change in lifestyle?
- How would you feel if you had to ask your children for money?
- How would you feel if you had to tell your children you couldn't fund their Ivy League education? If they had to attend an in-state college or university, would you consider that a tragedy?
- How would you feel if you had to tell your children that instead of a summer on an educational enrichment program traveling through Europe, they will have to work and earn money over the summer?

Legacy risks are also a concern:

- How would you feel if you were unable to fulfill your goals for leaving money to your heirs?
- Even worse, how would you feel if you became dependent on those heirs?

On *Longevity I*

On average, a woman turning 65 today will live more than 19.9 additional years, and a man more than 15.5 years.

On *Longevity II*

If I'd known I was going to live this long,
I would have taken better care of myself.
Eubie Blake, musician who is reported to have died at age 100

Especially with older clients, health-related risks are critical to consider and deal with appropriately:

- Is the risk of disability something you worry about?
- Have you thought about the risk of dying too soon?
- What happens if you live longer than you expected?
- Is the cost of health insurance a concern? What about the cost of long-term care?
- Are you concerned about your parents' health?
- Will they be able to take care of themselves financially and otherwise?
- How might your parents' aging or illness affect your life and financial plans?
- How about your grown children? Do they have health insurance? If not, what would you do if they needed care? How would that affect your financial future?

Lament of the Sandwich Generation

I'm 58 years old and trying to plan for my retirement. But my 85-year-old parents now are living with me, and my 32-year-old son just moved back in with us . . . with his kids.

Today's Sandwich Generation faces very real financial issues with their grown children and aging parents. Often, without the help of a great financial advisor, they are reluctant to face many of these issues, fail to deal with or plan for them, and end up with their own financial security in jeopardy. Consider this scenario. "I figured my 25-year-old daughter was old enough to take care of herself. I never thought to ask if her job with that start-up had health insurance. I learned it didn't right after the cancer diagnosis. You can't let your child get second-rate care, so I got out my checkbook. Thankfully, it's two years later and she's fine. But my pension plan is depleted, and the house is mortgaged again."

That parent found out the hard way the importance of getting the right kind of financial advice, guidance, and direction. Great financial advisors work with their clients on all aspects of risk and financial security. They help them understand and account for the downsides in life. As we've talked about throughout this book, those downsides can include:

- Unexpected losses
- Emotional decision making
- Inadequate planning
- Too aggressive or too conservative a stance in investment decisions
- Allowing fear and greed to dominate
- A lack of discipline
- Failing to rebalance a portfolio
- Allowing market conditions to dictate risk tolerance
- Maintaining the status quo because it's comfortable rather than diversifying

Once your clients sense that you are there to help them understand and protect them from the downsides and help them embrace the appropriate risks to preserve their vision of the future, you're well on your way to having clients for life. Their dreams and yours can come true.

THE TAKEAWAY

Great advisors:

- Recognize the importance of educating their clients about the various types of risk and how each can affect an individual's financial future
- Understand how and why their clients perceive risk
- Help their clients embrace risk adequately
- Work to protect their clients on both the downside and the upside
- Serve as the guardian of each of their clients' visions of their future
- Get their clients' emotions out of their investment and financial decisions

Chapter

6

GREAT QUESTIONS TO ASK

We've included this compilation of questions as a handy reference guide. It includes most of the questions in the book plus a few more. It is not intended as a complete list of all the questions you might ask a prospect or client. Rather, it is a list of the kinds of questions great financial advisors ask to get prospects to respect them and to cause clients to reveal the depth of information advisors need to do their job. Rather than organize these questions by the chapter in which they appear, we have organized them in a way we believe will be of the greatest use to you in working with prospects and clients.

GETTING THE FIRST APPOINTMENT

Nothing happens until you get the first appointment. When talking with a prospect on the telephone, be willing to get his or her attention by being unconventional. Here are a few examples of questions that can help:

1. You say you already have a financial advisor? Don't you think your financial future is worthy of a second opinion? Any good doctor will tell you to get a second opinion, right?
2. You say your financial advisor is doing a good job? Well, is "good" good enough for your financial future?
3. What would be your criteria for making a change? Is it better performance? More service? Fairer fees? Something else?
4. So, you're saying that you're "all set" and you don't need to meet with me? [Going on playfully] Wow, I'm not even sure where I'm going for dinner tonight but you're all set for your entire financial future. That's terrific. How were you able to accomplish that?
5. You say you like to pick your own stocks and you're good at it? How are you when it comes to risk management? How did you do in the last bear market?
6. How do you make investment decisions?
7. How good are you when it comes to selling stocks you hold? Do you have a "sell discipline"? What is it?
8. If I were to show you something clearly superior to what you are doing currently, would you make a change?
9. What is your portfolio designed to do?
10. Is there something about your finances you would like to improve?
11. Is there anything wrong with your current situation?
12. What is the best time of day for you to come in [for an appointment]? (After securing the appointment, but before ending the conversation, it usually makes sense to ask as many "data questions" as possible. The more you get up front, the more likely the first meeting will feel like a second meeting. Data questions include: What is your income? Assets? Location of various accounts?)

STARTING THE RELATIONSHIP

When a prospect comes into your office, don't start selling yourself or your services too soon. Instead, remember what medical doctors and other professionals tend to do. You might start with questions like these:

13. Can I help you?
14. How can I help you?
15. Why have you come in today?
16. Is their something that's concerning you today?
17. What has been your experience with money in the past?
18. How did you get to where you are today?
19. Why have you built your portfolio the way you have? Did someone help you? How did you go about it?

THE SURFACE ESSENTIALS

The following are the kinds of questions that generally should be answered at some point in your process. You might handle some of them with a questionnaire; others will be answered in response to the more open-ended questions that are included in the book and later in this section.

Objectives

20. What are you trying to accomplish?
21. What is important to you?
22. Have you determined your personal investment objectives?
23. Do you and your spouse or partner agree on those objectives?
24. Have you put your investment objectives in writing?
25. What is your biggest concern?

Portfolio

26. Why do you own that particular stock?
27. What is that fund doing for you?
28. Why are you so heavily invested in bonds?
29. What is the strategy behind your focus on [industry, sector, geographical region]?
30. Is there a reason why you don't have significant international holdings?
31. Do you consider your portfolio adequately diversified?

Assets, Liabilities, Income, and Expense

32. Where does your current income come from?
33. Do you have other sources of income? Trust fund? Alimony? Other?
34. Are you expecting an inheritance? From whom? Do you have any idea of a timetable?
35. Do you have any assets that currently provide or will provide an income?
36. What is your debt situation?
37. How do you spend your money?

Retirement and Education

38. When do you want to retire?
39. How much longer do you plan on working? How much longer do you wish to work?
40. Do you want to work during retirement? If so, full-time or part-time?
41. Do you feel you have done an adequate job funding your retirement?
42. Do you know what your income needs will be in today's dollars?

43. Do you know how much money you will need to give you the income you want and need in retirement?
44. Do you know how much you will have to set aside and what rate of return you will need to build your retirement nest egg?
45. Do you have a retirement plan at work?
46. Have you saved enough for your children's education?
47. Do your children have any special needs?

Investment Style

48. What kind of investor are you?
49. How involved do you want to be in your investments?
50. What are your primary sources of investment information and ideas?
51. Do you consider yourself a conservative or aggressive investor?
    - What does the phrase *conservative investor* mean to you?
    - What does the phrase *aggressive investor* mean to you?
52. When investing, do you like to strike out on your own or follow the crowd?
53. When you go on vacation, do you prefer to tour alone or go with a group?
54. Do you care more about how well you do in terms of dollars accrued or how you do compared with your friends and family?
55. Which is more important to you, beating the market or meeting your goals?

Planning Questions

56. Do you have a financial game plan?
57. How is your health?
58. When is the last time you reviewed your will and trusts?
59. Are your life and disability insurance adequate?

60. How prepared are you for a major catastrophe?
    - If a hurricane, earthquake, or another natural disaster occurred in your area, would you be positioned to deal with it financially?
    - Have you accounted in any way for the threat of terrorism in your financial plan?
61. Would your plan survive a major economic setback?
62. Is the risk of disability something you worry about?
63. What liability limits do you carry on your car insurance?
64. How much umbrella insurance coverage do you carry?
65. Have you thought about the risk of dying too soon?
66. If you live a long time, is there a risk you will run out of money or have to reduce your lifestyle?
67. What are your professional advisory relationships (your lawyers, accountants, others)? What services do they provide to you? How often do they communicate with you? Do you have confidence in them?

Starting to Look at Risk

68. What does risk mean to you?
69. What does risk tolerance mean to you?
70. What is your risk tolerance?
71. Can you rate your risk tolerance on a scale of 1 to 10?
72. To what degree are you willing to deal with a drop in your portfolio? What about repeated drops?
73. Looking at four alternative investment-return streams over five years, which would you prefer?

GOING DEEPER

Great financial advisors don't stop at the surface. They probe further and they use questions to do it. Here are some examples:

Experiences with Money, Success, and Failure

74. What was your biggest financial win? How did you feel about it?
75. Have you ever lost serious money? In other words, enough money to have affected your lifestyle, plans, or sleep?
76. Do you remember the first time you lost serious money? How did it happen and how did you respond?
77. What was your most painful financial mistake? How did you deal with it?
78. Have you, or anyone in your family, ever had a significant financial reversal?
    - A bankruptcy, loss of job, significant reduction in income or net worth?
    - At what stage of life did it occur?
    - What prompted the setback?
    - Whose fault was it?
    - How did it affect you?
79. What do you consider the major accomplishments of your life?
80. Have you ever had any major disappointments in your life as a child, in high school, and later in life?

Attitudes about Money

81. Are you rich? Do you feel rich? If not, how much money will make you feel rich?
82. In dollars, how much money would you like to have? When?
83. What does money mean to you?
84. Is money your first measure of someone's success?
85. Do you think money can make you happy?
86. Is there anything in your life experience, your relationships, your hopes, dreams, or fears that might affect your thoughts about money and investing?

Purpose and Goals

87. What do you want to do with your life?
88. Can you paint a picture of the way you want your future to look–a picture of your vision of your future? How would you feel if you achieved that vision? How would you feel if you didn't?
89. When you visualize your possible future, does anything concern or scare you?
90. What are you hoping your money will accomplish for you? Depending on the answer, you might ask, "Are you sure money will accomplish that?"
91. What benefits do you expect from money?
92. What does that goal (for example, "$3 million when I retire," "keeping our second home in Vail," or "a new top-of-the-line Lexus") really mean to you?
93. How long have you been thinking about this particular goal?
94. How do you think your life would change if you could snap your fingers and achieve that goal today?
95. Can you tell me what the underlying purpose is behind your goals?
96. What would have had to happen for you to consider our relationship a complete success?

Deeper into Risk

97. When it comes to money and your finances, what worries and concerns you? What about that worries you?
98. Does anything about money keep you up at night?
99. Do you regard financial risk solely as the loss of money?
    - Or do you consider lost opportunity a form of risk?
    - Is there some other form of risk that concerns you?
    - Which form of risk is most significant to you?

100. Which would make you feel worse? If you don't sell any of that $10 stock and the price drops to $5, or if you do sell and it goes up to $15?
101. Do you think that investment losses would affect your overall spirits, sleep habits, relationships, health, or work? In what way would those losses affect you? To what degree?
102. If we embark on a relationship today, how much money can we lose before you fire me?
    - You say you would fire me if you lost 10 percent, but what if the market was down 20 percent? Would you still fire me?
    - What if the market was up 10 percent and we were up only 5 percent? How would you feel then?
103. If your plan requires an *x* percent return per year for you to achieve your goals, would that be your only measure of success? If not, how else would you measure success?
104. What would you do if your job is eliminated or your expertise is devalued by technology or other changes in the economy?

Investment Style

105. How do you make investment decisions?
106. Does your appetite for risk change based on the environment?
107. Are you willing to take on more risk for something you truly need as opposed to something you merely want?
108. Are you willing to assume more risk with discretionary funds?
109. Do you and/or your spouse (or partner) ever go to a casino?
    - If so, why?
    - Which casino games do each of you like?
    - Do you gamble differently when you're ahead than when you're behind?

- Do you set limits on how much you're willing to lose?
- Do you set limits on how much you'll win before you quit?
- Do you quit when you said you would?

Probing Further

110. Is there something else?
111. Do you want to add anything?
112. Is there anything further?
113. Is there something more I should know?
114. Is there something you are not saying?

FAMILY MATTERS

Families are such an integral part of the process that they deserve questions of their own. Following are a number of examples:

Tell Me about Your Family

115. In what ways do you and your spouse or partner feel differently about money?
116. Do you and your spouse or partner see risk the same way or differently?
117. If either of you gamble, who is the more enthusiastic gambler?
118. Do you and your spouse (or partner) ever argue about money?
    - If so, what do you tend to disagree about?
    - Does it happen often?
    - How do you resolve your differences?

119. How do you handle money with your children?
    - Do you speak openly about money with your children or in their presence?
    - Do you give them an allowance?
    - Do they work for their allowance?
    - Have they ever had a job outside your home? Would you want them to?
120. Are your children enthralled with all the gambling on the Internet or with the poker craze?
    - Do you think they participate in any way?
    - How do you feel about that?
121. How is your and your spouse's (or partner's) health? Are your children well?
122. If your parents are alive, are you concerned about your parents' health?
123. How might your parents' aging or illness affect your life and financial plans?
    - Will your parents be able to take care of themselves financially and otherwise?
    - Is the cost of their health care a concern?
    - What about the cost of their long-term care?
    - Do you have siblings that will help with the costs and obligations?

Family Growing Up

124. Can you recall your earliest memory of money and investing?
125. Growing up, were you rewarded, punished, or loved with money?
126. What are your earliest recollections of money?
127. When you were a child, did you get an allowance? What chores, if any, did you do to get that allowance?
128. Did you have a job when you were in high school or college?
    - What did you do?
    - Do you remember how much you were paid?

129. Can you tell me about your parents and money?
    - Were they wealthy? Middle class? Working class? Poor?
    - How did they spend their money?
    - How did they feel about money?
    - Was their business life or career stable or volatile?
    - Did they move around a lot?
    - Are they still alive?
    - Did either of them gamble?
    - Has their attitude toward money changed over the years? In what way?

Parents and Family History

130. Has anyone in your family or close to you lost any serious money?
    - If so, how did that loss feel to you?
    - Did it affect your actions with regard to money?
131. What's the typical longevity in your family?
132. Are your parents still alive?
    - How old are they?
    - How old were they when they died?
    - How is/was your parents' health?

Family Obligations

133. What are your financial obligations to your family?
134. How would you feel if you were unable to fulfill your financial goals regarding your family?
135. How would you and your family emotionally handle a significant change in lifestyle?
136. How would you feel if you had to tell your children you couldn't fund their Ivy League education, and they would have to attend a state school?

137. How would you feel if you had to tell your children that instead of a summer on an educational enrichment program traveling through Europe, they will have to work and earn money over the summer?
138. How would you feel if you had to ask your children for money?

How About Your Grown Children?

139. Do they have health insurance?
    - If not, what would you do if they needed care?
    - How would that affect your financial future?

Planning on an Inheritance?

140. What is the risk it won't be what you think it will?
141. Is it possible that your parents will live long enough that any possible inheritance is depleted?

TAKING A STAND

Great advisors tell clients what they think, not what they think the client wants to hear. They take a stand. Here are some questions that cut to the chase:

When Addressing . . .

142. A person who is unrealistic about investing for or in retirement:
    - How will it feel when you have to go back to work?

143. A person about to make a huge mistake:
    - Do you want me to respond professionally? Or would you prefer that I tell you how I really think?
144. People with all their eggs in one basket:
    - What's the point of all this concentration?
    - What if the stock craters?
    - What makes that vacation home so important to you?
    - To what end are you taking all this risk?
    - If I gave you a check for the full value of your entire position, do you think you would really invest it all in that one place? Wouldn't you diversify at least some of it?
    - What if the competitive landscape shifts dramatically for your business?
    - What if the real estate cycle turns again?
    - What if an Enron buys the company and milks it dry?
    - What if technology makes its basic product obsolete?
    - What if the bottom falls out of the industry, as happened to the airline industry after 9/11?
145. Mr. Cocky, Paul Perfect, or the Hobbyist:
    - Does your investment process live up to your claims?
146. A Hobbyist or the Putterer:
    - Wouldn't you rather be doing something else?
    - Would you hire a money manager who says the reason he or she manages money is to keep busy?
    - Doesn't your financial future deserve more?
    - Doesn't your financial future deserve professional help?
    - If you could choose a money manager from among ten people–nine of the best professional money managers in the industry and you–would you pick yourself? Would anyone?
    - Do you grow your own food? Raise your own meat? Sew your own clothing? Build your own house? Mow your own lawn? Prepare your own taxes?

147. The Cynic:
    - Who do you trust? Your accountant? Your doctor?
    - Did you have a bad experience with an advisor in the past?
    - Is there anything I can say or do to allay your concerns?
    - When it comes to working with advisors, do you consider yourself a realist, a cynic, or something else?
    - What happened to make you so cynical?
148. The Controller:
    - If you planted a garden and examined the roots every day, what would happen to your vegetables?
149. Paul Perfect:
    - Where are your various advisors falling down on the job?
    - What aren't they doing for you?
    - Are they doing anything that you feel is unsatisfactory or less than perfect?
    - Is there anything someone else might do better?
150. The Analytic:
    - What do you think the purpose of investment analysis actually is?
151. Ms. Pennywise:
    - I'm proud of my fees. May I explain why?
    - If the fee was more to your liking, would you be ready for us to start working together on your affairs?
    - Do you have the same high-quality expertise as a team of professionals?
    - How much is your time worth on a per-hour basis?
    - What's the total cost if you do it yourself?
    - Do you think a team of professionals can achieve a better return than you?
    - Do you think that as a professional advisor I would be able to either increase your return or protect you from making a mistake that would cost you more than the amount of my fee?
    - Would you rather get Lasik eye surgery from the cut-rate corner shop or from a top-notch ophthalmologist?

Risk

152. How can I help you so you will never be afraid to open your mail and read your statements?
153. What if your assets, your income, and your expertise all lose their value at the same time?
154. How would you feel if you lost 25 percent of your capital?
155. How would you feel if your beach house were destroyed and along with it a huge chunk of your assets?

Questions That Get to the Next Step

156. Do you see the logic of what we've outlined here today?
157. Does the process make sense to you?
158. Do you have a clear sense of what our working relationship would be like?
159. Are you satisfied that it can work for you over time?
160. Do you understand that if we start the process today, the platform is flexible and we can make adjustments as we go along?
161. Are you comfortable with the process and the plan?
162. Do you see the need for any adjustments to meet your specific needs?
163. Do you see how what we've outlined is better than what you're currently doing?
164. I don't see any reason why we shouldn't proceed. Do you?
165. Is there anything you need to know before we take the next step?
166. Is something keeping you from starting a relationship now?
167. Is there anything you need to do before we can start working together?
168. Is there a problem in telling your existing advisor that you're making a change? Is there anything I can do to make that easier for you?

169. Are there others in your family or professional advisory team you would like me to meet with to make you more comfortable with proceeding?
170. Will you empower me to be the guardian of your long-term financial future?

When You Must . . .

171. May I be brutally frank with you?
172. Can I be completely honest with you?
173. Can we be blunt with each other?

Referral Questions

174. Do you have any friends or colleagues who are dealing with some of the same things we have been discussing who might benefit from a meeting with me?
175. How would you describe my services to a friend?
176. Do you have any concerns about referring me to your friends and colleagues? Is there anything I can do to alleviate those concerns?

Four of Our Favorite Questions

177. Who do you want my primary client to be? Who should I stand up for? You now? You later? Your heirs?
178. Do you see how conservative can actually be aggressive and vice versa?
179. ____________________? [The pause and a glance as a question]
180. Do you know what you should do?

Got Questions? Want More Questions?

Log on to *www.parisse.com* and click on The Question Exchange.

Post yours, read theirs.

Index